# BLACKS
# IN
# WHITE-COLLAR
# JOBS

# BLACKS
# IN
# WHITE-COLLAR
# JOBS

**BRIAN J. O'CONNELL**

Landmark Studies

**ALLANHELD OSMUN** Montclair **UNIVERSE BOOKS** New York

**ALLANHELD, OSMUN & CO. PUBLISHERS, INC.**
**19 Brunswick Road, Montclair, New Jersey 07042**

Published in the United States of America in 1979
by Allanheld, Osmun & Co. and by Universe Books
381 Park Avenue South, New York, New York 10016
Distribution: Universe Books

LIBRARY OF CONGRESS CATALOGING IN PUBLICATION DATA
O'Connell, Brian J.
    Blacks in white-collar jobs.

    "Landmark studies."
    Bibliography: p.
    Includes index.
    1.   White collar workers—United States.
2.  Afro-Americans—Employment.  3.  Cities and
towns—United States.  I.  Title
HD8039.M4U567      331.6'3'96073      78-71098
ISBN 0-87663-838-8

Printed in the United States of America

*In loving memory of
my Mom and Dad*

# Contents

# List of Tables

Table

Appendix Table

# Preface

In 1969, I could see massive new office structures rising in Manhattan from the windows of the high school in which I taught in Bedford-Stuyvesant. There were about 60 new office buildings under construction at that time containing enough rentable space to cover over 1,100 football fields. But I could count the new construction projects in Bedford-Stuyvesant on the fingers of one hand, and the largest of these was a police precinct house. This was despite the fact that many blocks of this largest concentration of blacks in the country were leveled awaiting the promised (and still mostly undelivered) Model Cities housing.

While I regretted this apparently unequal allocation of both public and private resources, I recognized there was another side to the coin. The construction, office, and service jobs resulting from this office construction boom were important sources of income for Bedford-Stuyvesant residents struggling to become self-sufficient. Despite the prosperity of the late 1960s, there was no great expansion in most blue-collar job categories, and in the New York area, there was a decline. But for every blue-collar job lost at that time in New York, there was one white-collar job gained. The neighborhood activists paid little attention to the job supply issue.

The questions arising from this experience inspired my dissertation (*The Impact of Central Business District Renewal on Black Employment,* Ohio State University, 1974). Since then, I continued data gathering and analysis on the detailed occupational patterns in the central business district which appear in Chapter 5 of this volume, on residential centrality which appears in Chapters 3 and 7, and on workplace and residence data for whites and blacks which appear in the treatment of the mismatch hypothesis in Chapter 4. I have also added much theoretical material from the labor market literature, which in turn has helped to sharpen and refine the data analysis. In this, I feel part of a fortunate trend in which economists, sociologists, and planners are cooperating to link labor market, stratification, and residential land-use models to the mutual enrichment of each.

My largest debt of thanks is due to Professor Kent P. Schwirian in the Sociology Department at Ohio State University. His advice, given in generous amounts of his time over the last seven years, was constructive and challenging. Professors Edward C. McDonagh and Russell R. Dynes of the Sociology Department and Professor Frederick D. Stocker of the Economics Department at Ohio State University offered advice and encouragement at various stages of the research. Forrest Williams, a staff member in the Polimetrics Laboratory at Ohio State University, assisted in the process of accessing information from the computer tapes of the Public Use Sample of the Bureau of the Census. Anthony Scarnati of the Department of Sociology and Anthropology at St. John's University assisted in the task of gathering and calculating data. Professor Karl E. Taeuber of the Institute for Research on Poverty at the University of Wisconsin graciously offered the use of the indexes of residential segregation prepared by the Institute. The Department of Sociology and the Polimetrics Laboratory at Ohio State University made research facilities available for my use both for the doctoral and post-doctoral research. Valuable assistance was offered by Marie Rogers with the typing and by Phyllis Zumato in the typing, proofing, and assembling of the manuscript.

# Introduction

"Our ancestors made it, why can't they?" This question or accusation has often been posed by the descendants of European immigrants to American cities as they analyze the experience of the recent migrants, particularly many of the blacks who are not economically self-sufficient. In the attempt to put the onus on individuals, the assumption is made that the recent migrants are entering the same kind of labor market that the European immigrants of the nineteenth and early twentieth centuries entered.

The earlier groups entered urban labor markets that had expanding blue-collar sectors with many entry-level jobs available. The immigrants and their descendants were assimilated fairly quickly because there were expanding job opportunities at all levels of the social ladder. Blacks entered the cities when most job openings were replacement openings rather than new positions. Almost all of the expansion was in the white-collar sector. Blacks moved near the central business districts (hereafter CBD) of the largest cities, where blue-collar jobs were disappearing and a disproportionate share of white-collar jobs were concentrating. The black migration and the office expansion of the CBD were largely coincidental, but the subsequent assimilation of blacks into the labor market depended in part on whether they were getting a foothold in the easily accessible CBD labor market.

The blacks did get a foothold, but because of the nature of many of the office and office-associated jobs that became available, it was a very tenuous foothold. Many of the ordinary clerical and service jobs created in this office expansion did not offer high wages, advancement opportunities, union protection, or stability. But neither did these jobs score so low on these characteristics that they could be classified as secondary or peripheral jobs confined to the poor. Various theories, such as the dual labor market theory[1] and theories which recognize a larger number of labor market segments with varying degrees and combinations of these characteristics[2] will be explored in this study.

The economic assimilation of blacks is entering a new phase. Migration has slowed significantly. Since most job openings in the last quarter of this century are in white-collar positions, blacks are facing a different pathway to assimilation than earlier migrants. The job opportunities in the whole economy, and particularly in the CBD, are not being spread equally in the black community. Women and better educated young blacks find better opportunities. Education is having a pay-off for blacks who acquire white-collar skills. Those with poor educational backgrounds are facing a difficult time in the labor market. This may lead to intensified class division among blacks. Black women are finding job opportunities which satisfy some of their expectations, but which will not bring a lot of wealth into the black community. White women are often very satisfied with these same opportunities where the incomes supplement the income of the family's principal breadwinner. But in black families where the income of the husband is inadequate or the husband is not present, the women will not be satisfied. Young black males are finding some opportunities in the CBD, but there is extreme competition. The experience of the different sexes in the job market could lead to increased family strains.

While the primary concern in this study is the black experience in the CBD labor market, much attention will be given to the changes taking place in the CBD. This is to set a context for the study of black labor and to show the impact of decisions regarding downtown development on the labor market.

Despite dire predictions from many quarters, the central

business districts of our larger cities are alive and thriving. The prophets of gloom cite a list of faults of CBDs which is long and morbid, but these districts are not falling over and playing dead. Their skylines are mushrooming with skyscrapers. New office structures predominate, but new convention centers, hotels, arenas, shops, and in some cities, housing appear among or close to the new office buildings.

Large-scale developments often serve as focal points which draw and inspire other building. Peachtree Center in Atlanta, Embarcadero Center in San Francisco, The Charles Center in Baltimore, Houston Center, Nicollet Mall in Minneapolis, the Superdome in New Orleans, the Renaissance Center in Detroit, and the Crown Center in Kansas City are centerpieces of extensive downtown renewal. Older downtowns that had seen little building for decades like Chicago, Philadelphia, and Boston have new skylines in the last 15 years. Even Los Angeles, which is often cited as a model for decentralized urban development, has a new cluster of tall buildings in the Bunker Hill area.

Various questions are raised about this surge of building. Does this physical construction, by itself, indicate vitality? Is the quality of much of the glass box architecture sterile and uninspiring? Is downtown renewal using resources that could be better spent on the renewal of other parts of the city, particularly inner-city housing? Are there positive externalities in downtown redevelopment that overflow to other parts of the city? Does a renewed central business district provide jobs, especially for the minorities who live close to it? Is it adding to the "mismatch" whereby high-skilled jobs are placed near the residences of low-skilled workers?

This study focuses on some of the latter questions. It specifically looks at the impact of CBD employment patterns on the black labor force. It investigates whether the office or office-associated jobs which are so predominant in the renewed CBD are a boon or a bane to blacks.

The 1970 U.S. Census for the first time has delineated the CBD as a place of work and, accordingly, has tabulated many important data items. This offers the first opportunity to study CBD labor markets with any intensity, even though research must be done on a cross-sectional rather than a longitudinal basis. Most studies on the CBD to date have used only indirect measures of CBD employment. The number counted entering the CBD on a workday has been used by those studying urban transportation.[3] Many studies simply *inferred* what was happening in the CBD from employment statistics for the *whole* central city. The only direct study of CBD jobs or job loss to this author's knowledge is a study on workers covered by unemployment compensation by postal zones in the city of Chicago.[4] The present research uses data on CBD employment in 54 of the largest American cities to study the impact of CBD change.

## Notes

1. See Michael J. Piore, "The Dual Labor Market: Theory and Implications," in *Problems in Political Economy: An Urban Perspective*, ed. D. M. Gordon (Lexington, Mass.: D.C. Heath, 1971), pp. 90–94.

2. See Marcia Freedman, *Labor Markets: Segments and Shelters* (Montclair, N.J.: Allanheld, Osmun & Co. Publishers, 1976).

3. J. R. Meyer, J. F. Kain, and M. Wohl, *The Urban Transportation Problem* (Cambridge: Harvard University Press, 1965), pp. 35–39.

4. John F. Kain, "The Distribution and Movement of Jobs and Industry," in *The Metropolitan Enigma*, ed. James Wilson (Cambridge: Harvard University Press, 1968), pp. 23–24.

# 1    Office Growth and Black Employment

## The Growth of Offices in the CBD

The black migration to the central cities took place in the context of office expansion and the decline of blue-collar occupations in those central cities. Office jobs were centralizing in the city, while the territorial trend for blue-collar jobs was decentralization or suburbanization. Although there are some indications that office jobs might follow the pattern of the blue-collar jobs, the warning signs have been exaggerated. Significant changes are not on the horizon.

The percentage of clerical jobs in the labor force is continuing to expand, providing the foundation for more growth in CBD offices. John Kasarda found that as various types of social systems get larger, they require a higher proportion of people in clerical jobs.[1] The proportionate increase in clerical jobs is even greater than the increase in managerial, professional, or technical jobs. So as the economy is expanding, more clerical help is in demand. Max Carey estimates that the clerical work force will increase by 34 percent between 1974 and 1985, while the total labor force will grow by only 20 percent.[2]

Regina Armstrong has prepared an extensive study of the office industry in the United States.[3] In a 12-year period from 1957 to 1968, she found that the growth rate in office space was about 5 percent annually. Office-type occupations increased from 30 to almost 40 percent of all jobs in the United States between 1950 and 1970.

A large proportion of this growth was in the CBDs of our largest cities. Manhattan increased its office space 80 percent from 1950 to 1970, while the Dallas CBD increased its office space 200 percent in the same period. The largest cities had a disproportionate share of this office activity. In 1960, the 100 largest metropolitan areas had 64 percent of all office-type occupations, but only 54 percent of the nation's population. The 24 cities with population over one million had 43 percent of office jobs compared to 34 percent of the nation's population.[4]

Armstrong traced the history of office growth in three components: the headquarters component—serving national or international markets; the middle market component—serving regional markets in excess of 150,000 population; and the local market component—serving communities with less than 150,000 people. The larger cities draw the headquarters component. Armstrong finds a "critical mass" of central office employment is achieved in certain cities where a self-sustaining or self-attracting growth in headquarters firms takes hold. These cities have an infrastructure that provides for easy interaction between firms, highly skilled labor markets, complementary ancillary business services, and prestige for image-conscious firms. In the larger cities, she does not find any strict correlation between population size and office activity. The "surplus" office activity of some cities represents their specialization in office work for the headquarters component. In the middle market component, Armstrong finds that the need of companies for a sizeable white-collar labor pool is a constraint on their freedom to move away from central cities. Some of the jobs, however do leave the larger cities to go to intermediate size cities.[5]

In a noted essay on the economic development of cities, E. E. Lampard cites a principle that "specialization will thrive best where it is most developed."[6] Boris Yavitz and Thomas Stanback demonstrate how new jobs in one sector of the office industry generate new income, and in turn, new capital for development.[7] They estimated the multiplier effect for new jobs in data processing in New York. They find that for each new job in data processing, one other job is created in the city.

Great publicity has been given to the exodus of headquarter offices from the city, particularly from Manhattan. This trend must be seen in its proper perspective. First, it is rare that a company abandons its office in the core. Often, as in the case of IBM, only a fraction of the Manhattan office is moved. When IBM moved 1,000 workers to its new headquarters in Armonk, N.Y., it left 6,700 workers behind in the Manhattan office.[8] GE, Coca Cola, AT&T, and many other companies followed the same pattern. "Executive offices" might be a better name for the new suburban units than "front office" or "head-quarters." It is common that large companies have different office locations in the CBD for their different functions: executive offices, credit departments, data processing, export offices, and operating divisions. Often only one of these units leaves the CBD.

Second, only a handful of the companies that transferred offices from Manhattan have moved out of the New York metropolitan area. Wolfgang Quante studied the headquarters movements of the Fortune 500 and found that 44 of the 144 located in Manhattan in 1956 had left, but 70 percent of them moved to the New York suburbs. They did not move far enough to cut the umbilical cord to Manhattan. Quante found another movement that has received little publicity, namely, that 15 of the Fortune 500 moved to Manhattan.[9]

Third, while some sectors of office activity like the securities and industrial corporate headquarters have declined, other sectors have more than compensated for the loss. Matthew Drennan found that many of the corporations that left Manhattan continued to use the same New York City service firms—banks, law firms, accountants, communications, transportation, and real estate. Offices for foreign companies have also been expanding rapidly in Manhattan.[10]

Fourth, the trend in New York does not represent the trend for the country. Many of the company headquarters which left the New York metropolitan area have relocated in CBDs in other cities. Central business districts across the country have seen much office growth. Many offices, particularly from the local office component, have located in suburbs across the country. Some people seeing new offices in the suburbs conclude that these offices left the CBD. But the growth in office employment has been large enough to sustain a growth in both CBD and suburb.

Finally, market forces and other forms of resistance slow the move to the suburbs. Suburbs have found that offices do not bring the cornucopia of benefits that were anticipated. They have required expensive new services and have brought new traffic problems. Some suburban areas are refusing to rezone land for office use. Rental costs for office space in the CBD and the suburbs around New York equalized, although it is uncertain whether this was the result of cost equalization forcing suburban rents upward, or whether the oversupply in Manhattan after the construction of 61 million square feet of office space (the equivalent of 1,355 football fields) from 1969 through 1974 forced Manhattan rents downward.[11] Nationally, Gerald Manners finds that CBD office locations have cost advantages over suburban locations with a few exceptions.[12] Large office units find it is difficult to recruit large numbers of clerical workers to one location in the suburbs. Edgar Hoover and Raymond Vernon found that offices with staffs of over 500 have difficulty recruiting labor even in the New York suburbs.[13]

The total picture that emerges is that the New York CBD has experienced an exodus of office units but not to any alarming degree. There is no reason to suspect that the trend will seriously affect the other CBDs in the country.

## Government Renewal Efforts

Urban Renewal started as an effort to improve housing, but eventually a larger share of renewal funds went into downtown commercial development. The housing programs of the New Deal and the Housing Act of 1949 were aimed specifically at improving the supply of housing and slum clearance. In 1954, the Housing Act was amended by the Workable Program, which was written to increase the contributions of private enterprise and to demand more local participation in planning.

Subtle changes appeared in the program. In 1954, 10 percent

of Urban Renewal funds could be spent on land which was not used for residential purposes either before or after the renewal. The "before or after" provision allowed part of the other 90 percent to be used to convert residential land to non-residential uses. In a 1961 amendment to the Housing Act, 30 percent of the money was allowed to be used for renewal in areas that were not residential either before or after renewal. Scott Greer and Lowdon Wingo note that "blight clearance" was used in the legislation rather than "slum clearance."[14] The two might appear synonymous, but they are not. "Blight" was defined so loosely that it came to mean any property which could be rebuilt for a "higher" use. The "higher" use might be better housing or commercial use with a higher property evaluation.

Harold Kaplan traces the history of urban renewal in Newark, N.J., which is a typical case history.[15] For nine years after the 1949 Housing Act, Newark officials tried but could not put together any significant housing renewal programs in the slums. Developers were not interested and the terms of the law made FHA mortgage insurance difficult to obtain. Finally, city officials worked directly with developers to pick sites. The office of the Urban Renewal Administration in Washington could not publicly condone the selection of redevelopers before the site selection, but it turned its back on the practice. These developers with government seed money chose sites, not in the heart of the ghetto, but on the border of the CBD. They took run-down commercial and residential areas, using the right of emminent domain to clear areas as big as 15 blocks. The renewed areas contained luxury apartments, offices, and stores. Once one or two large urban renewal projects took place, it made it profitable for developers to start nearby, perhaps with less or no Urban Renewal help.

The net effect of this pattern of development before 1960 is that while 85 percent of the areas certified for clearance were residential before renewal, 50 percent were commercial after renewal.[16] Martin Anderson notes that by 1961, 126,000 dwelling units were destroyed in Urban Renewal projects, including 25,000 "standard" units that happened to be in designated areas.[17] In their places, only 25,000 new units were built. A Department of Housing and Urban Development study revealed that of 60,000 small businesses dislocated by

Urban Renewal projects, 20,000 liquidated instead of moving.[18] Thus, housing residents and small businesses have lost out, while developers and large commercial interests have profited by the program. Much of this renewal has been in or near the CBD. These patterns continued until the "New Federalism" of Nixon displaced Urban Renewal.

Judith Friedman found that cities which ranked high on the amount of office activity had larger numbers of Urban Renewal programs than those that ranked low.[19] This suggests that Urban Renewal had its greatest impact around CBD office centers.

It cannot be said for certain how much CBD renewal has depended on Urban Renewal money. Hoover and Vernon trace the evolution of residential neighborhoods through downgrading and renewal stages.[20] They note that the last stage, renewal, depends to a large extent on government intervention, rather than a normal combination of ecological and demographic trends. The parallel with CBD renewal may not be exact, but it is safe to say that CBD renewal of the 1950s and the early 1960s would not have taken place as quickly or extensively without Urban Renewal. Offices would have been built, but not necessarily in the CBD.

Patterns of government involvement have been less clear since the advent of Nixon's New Federalism and the Community Block Grant program. There has been much heralding of the fact that centers like the Renaissance Center and the Embarcadero Center have been built mostly with private capital. But the government has been involved through land preparation, subsidy, tax abatement, and many other ways. The developers, real estate interests, and companies who fostered the earlier downtown developments have their lobbyists, their financial connections, and their knowledge mobilized to shape state and city legislation. Many people welcome this new interest of private business in the CBD. As state and local governments involve themselves further with these downtown renewal efforts, they ought to search out the consequences, particularly the impact on the employment and income of the people. Local neighborhood groups often oppose CBD development programs in the fight for scarce government money. But they, too, must analyze the importance of job centers for the people.

Robert Fitch would have us look, not at the planners or politicians, but at the businessmen when trying to understand the allocation of resources for office development in CBDs like Manhattan.[21] Since New York was bound to lose some of its manufacturing, food processing, and shipping industries, Fitch maintains that the business and financial people determined to get their share of the surplus value produced nationally and internationally in the form of rents, mortgages, construction loans on high-rise office buildings, and in the appreciation of the world's highest land values. They made credit available for the projects they favored, and they funded the Regional Plan Association to design and propose the kind of development that would make New York a national and international office center. It remains to be proven whether regional and national office centers will inevitably emerge, or whether they emerge only through the collusion of financial leaders as Fitch contends. Whether Fitch's theory is accepted in full or not, he does make us aware of another causative variable that cannot be ignored. The role of business and financial leaders is too often underestimated in this process.

## Opinions About the CBD and Black Employment

There are many shades of opinion regarding the impact of CBD renewal on black employment. Larry Orr is one of the more recent in a long line of researchers who have demonstrated that low-income workers tend to live closer to their places of work.[22] There is ample evidence to highlight the importance of CBD labor market change on inner-city residents.

On the pessimistic side, a popular view is captured in the words of a New York City insurance executive, "You can't get good clerical people. You can get bodies, but for proper help you have to go where they have gone—to the suburbs."[23] Wolfgang Quante reports on an Economic Development Council study of 108 large clerical firms in New York. Half of the companies complained that not enough clerical help was available in Manhattan, and 70 percent complained that the quality was poor.[24]

The racial factor gets mixed in with the competence factor. This New York executive might have been thinking that blacks and Puerto Ricans make up 40 percent of present labor force entrants, and 62 percent of the students in the New York City public schools. A similar situation occurs to some degree in most large cities.

Various writers take the position that office development has been the salvation of the CBD and the labor market of the city. One example is Lawrence Alexander, the editor of the *Downtown Idea Exchange*. In advising planners on how to win support for downtown projects, he said, "Talk about the jobs created and supplied downtown."[25] Similar claims appear in the planning literature, often with the comment that without CBD renewal, the job position of the inner-city minorities would be even worse.

Recent studies of black employment in clerical occupations offer optimistic viewpoints on blacks' getting clerical jobs in the CBD. As evidence of the dramatic change between 1960 and 1970, the proportion of black workers in white-collar jobs in New York City rose from 29 percent to 43 percent. The percentage for black women jumped from 32 percent to 55 percent.[26] Michael Flax found the same pattern with national data. In fact, if the 1960 to 1968 rate of change continued, the proportion of blacks in white-collar jobs would have been the same as the corresponding proportion of whites according to Flax's calculations.[27] Stuart Garfinkle found that the percentage of clerical workers who were black increased from 5.1 percent to 9.4 percent between 1962 and 1974.[28] Dale Hiestand shows that in New York, blacks had achieved 88 percent of parity with whites among clerical workers by 1970 (where 100 percent would indicate that blacks had the same percentage employed in clerical jobs as whites).[29]

This rapid movement of black workers into clerical positions may affect residential and class patterns. Eugene Uyeki found that clerical workers were the least segregated residentially of the different categories of workers.[30] While cause and effect are not clear, as more blacks get clerical jobs there may be less residential segregation. There was evidence that black income parity with whites rose significantly in the 1960s. It rose from 52 percent of parity to 64 percent of parity.[31] This is partially connected to the increase of black participation in white-collar jobs. The data on CBD workers will give detailed information on black participation in the CBD labor force.

There are two closely related bodies of literature which address the issue of jobs for central city residents. One is the literature on the mismatch hypothesis, the other is the literature on the suburbanization of jobs. The mismatch hypothesis postulates that the semi-skilled and unskilled jobs which central city residents are best equipped to fill are moving to the suburbs, while the job openings in the central city demand greater competence than the residents there possess.

Raymond Vernon was one of the first to point to this mismatch in his study of the changing economic function of the central city in the 1950s.[32] While most of the recent research on the question casts doubt or adds qualifiers to the hypothesis, Bennett Harrison offers examples of the "ubiquity of this assumption in discussions of urban policy."[33] Programs like reverse transportation (busing from an inner-city ghetto to a suburban factory area) were built on the assumption that this hypothesis was true.

The mismatch hypothesis itself is founded upon many assumptions. Charles Brecher challenged some of these assumptions.[34] One possibly faulty assumption is that the service jobs opening up in the central city are mostly highly skilled jobs for which few blacks are qualified. Another is that blacks lack education and skills. Brecher points out that the typical black worker in the central city is at least a high school graduate. There are other doubtful assumptions, especially regarding the level of competition for central city jobs, that will be explored in more detail in Chapter 4. Previous research on the mismatch hypothesis has not separated the experiences of black and white workers, and it is not safe to assume that the experiences of both have been the same.

The research on the suburbanization of jobs did examine its impact on blacks. John Kain reasoned that the distance from black residential areas to many jobs helped to explain the data he had linking low levels of black employment and housing segregation.[35] Travel costs, lack of information about distant jobs, and the fears of employers about bringing blacks into predominantly white areas combine to keep blacks out of certain labor markets.

Joseph Mooney went a step further in attempting to show that the mismatch between central city residence and suburban job locations was empirically verifiable. By using the ratio of central city jobs to SMSA (Standard Metropolitan Statistical Area) jobs and the proportion of blacks living in the central city but working outside it, he did find a link between the suburbanization of jobs and the level of central city unemployment.[36] The evidence was clearer for black men than for black women. Stanley Friedlander found similar results in his study.[37]

Stanley Masters did not find evidence that the suburbanization of jobs affected black-white income ratios.[38] His finding does not directly contradict the Kain-Mooney hypothesis that the suburbanization of jobs affects black employment levels, but it does complicate the issue. Masters has not tested alternative explanations for his finding, but he suggests the possibilities that central city jobs are better paid than suburban ones due to tight central city labor markets, or that blacks are getting some quality suburban jobs.

Bennett Harrison focused on the employment characteristics of blacks living in the core of cities, in the rest of the central cities, and in the suburbs.[39] He showed that the unemployment rate of male blacks living in the cores was substantially higher than the other two residential groups of blacks. There was little difference among the three black male residential groups on median earnings, and no difference on median occupational status. This follows the pattern of research on the suburbanization of jobs which had found that unemployment rates were affected more than earnings rates.

Harrison noted that the black experience was quite different from the white experience. Suburban whites had significantly better earnings and occupational status than their central city counterparts. The black suburbanites did not have this advantage over their central city counterparts. Harrison concluded that urban blacks were severely constrained in their search for employment no matter where they lived in the metropolis, and that policies designed to rearrange the intra-metropolitan configuration of black residences would do little to improve their employment prospects. Harrison did not look specifically at job location, but assumed that people would profit from nearby job sources. Chapter 4 of this study will look at racial distribution by both residence and job location.

In examining the black employment experience in the city, the analyst should not assume that a white-collar job is a stepping stone on the road to success. For the earlier European immigrant, the white-collar job was a sign of achievement, but many of the circumstances have changed.

Many of the white-collar jobs created in the last quarter of the century must be looked at in a new light. Marcia Freedman found various segments of the labor market differentiated by levels of job stability, access to promotion ladders, earnings, and union protection. She found office clericals to be quite similar in these characteristics across various types of industries. Generally they were at a fairly low level of earnings and stability.[40]

There are studies which show the relatively inferior quality of office clerical jobs, which account for the biggest proportion of growth in white-collar jobs. Harry Braverman points to an increasing division of labor in the office, more repetition, and more mindless work.[41] The division of labor is done in such a way that required levels of skill are not increased, but decreased. The computerization and mechanization of office functions turns the great mass of office workers into mindless attendants rather than operators or managers of the process. In short, the office is becoming more like a factory. Braverman views the situation quite pessimistically. In a Marxian framework, he sees the alienation of work spreading to office jobs. He offers much concrete data to support his theory, but the validity of his interpretation remains controversial.

Louise Kapp Howe delineates a process by which female office workers are kept out of promotional channels.[42] The good office worker follows orders rather than gives them, and is a good detail person rather than a creative person. The very qualities that make good office workers are the opposite of those that would qualify them for advancement.

Braverman's and Howe's contentions have many implications. First, office jobs are not necessarily avenues to great success for their holders, nor do they bring great wealth. But as entry level jobs for recent migrants and their children, they may serve the same function as factory jobs did for earlier immigrants. From the employers' point of view, it may be to their advantage not to have highly educated, ambitious people in these jobs. As long as a certain minimimum skill and reliability level is reached, the office employers might be quite content with the labor supply of the central city. There are many sides to the issue, some optimistic and some pessimistic for blacks.

Only three out of ten jobs added in the private sector of the economy since 1950 have been good jobs, according to Eli Ginzberg.[43] Most of the new jobs paid below the average weekly earnings of all Americans. Many of these new jobs, of course, were clerical jobs filled by women. In light of this, Ginzberg asks why there has been so little criticism and discontent among Americans who obtained these jobs. He says that the most plausible reason is that most of these workers were not the primary breadwinners in the family, but the secondary bread-winners. They were happy to have the extra income. Ginzberg does not differentiate among blacks and whites. Among blacks, when the husband is underemployed or when the woman is the head of the household, the income is not just supplemental. These white-collar job opportunities serve quite different functions in the white and black communities.

## Theoretical and Practical Implications

Some urban planners argue for a strong core for the city, a "heart" that provides life blood to the rest of the city. This is the centrist school. There are ecological, cultural, and transportation factors involved, but an important part of their argument is that the "heart" pumps needed blood into the city in the form of jobs and income. The centrist school will be examined in the next chapter.

Some urban economists have evolved functional classification schemes for cities, and suggest that only certain types of cities can efficiently invest large amounts of their resources into central business district renewal. The next chapter will also examine this theory, especially from the viewpoint of the employment advantages for blacks.

It is difficult to understand urban employment patterns, and it is similarly difficult to understand residential patterns. The sociologists who developed the classical ecological models of urban development (the concentric circle model, the sector model, and the multiple nuclei model) originally included both labor market and residential factors. Sociological research has emphasized the residential patterns in recent years; but changes in the metropolis make it imperative to give more attention to the labor market, and challenge two assumptions in these models. One challenge is that the CBD's economic function is changing. The other is that there is no large new immigrant group moving into the bottom rung of the social ladder in the cities to replace the blacks or Hispanics who are there now. This immigrant flow was a triggering mechanism for the expansion process in all three models. Any adapted model would have to analyze CBD employment and its employment opportunities for inner-city minorities.

Further CBD employment change may help determine whether inner-city poverty areas will continue to thin out, whether there will be a return of the middle and upper classes to the area around the CBD, or whether the inner-city poverty area will remain as it is with the poor trapped by a chain of interaction effects between residential, employment, and educational factors. These possibilities will be examined within the context of the classic urban ecological models in the next chapter.

Finally, at the risk of oversimplification, two different scenarios will be offered here showing possible courses of events as blacks try to enter the economic mainstream:

1) The assimilation of blacks into the urban labor force is severely hampered by the switch from blue-collar to white-collar jobs. With the many other disadvantages the blacks have, the impossibility of getting a strong foothold in the expanding white-collar sector keeps them locked on the periphery of the labor market.

2) The expanding white-collar sector is serving the same function now for the blacks that the blue-collar sector provided for the earlier immigrants. While the advancement will not be quick, these jobs provide a foundation for further intergenerational advancement. But two aspects of this white-collar employment may cause disruption or division in the black community and family. The black woman may fare better in

the urban labor market than black men. Second, there may be increasing class division among blacks as some have the skills to get white-collar jobs and others do not.

The first of these scenarios reflects the simple version of the dual labor market theory. The second reflects the theory that recognizes multiple labor market segments, but with refinements. The refinements include a historical pattern of change in the labor market structure that affects immigrants or migrants of succeeding time periods in different ways. The refinements also include a differential impact on black men and black women. In addition, the second scenario borrows an element from the dual labor market theory in that some people are left out of the economic mainstream. But this will bring increasing class division among blacks as some get absorbed into the labor market and others find themselves locked out of it. The remaining chapters will consider which of these scenarios is more likely to become a reality.

## Notes

1. John D. Kasarda, "The Structural Implications of Social System Size," *American Sociological Review* 39 (February 1974).

2. Max L. Carey, "Revised Occupational Projections to 1985," *Monthly Labor Review* (November 1976), p. 13.

3. Regina Belz Armstrong, *The Office Industry: Patterns of Growth and Location* (Cambridge: M.I.T. Press, 1972).

4. *Ibid.*, pp. 13–23.

5. *Ibid.*, pp. 19–30.

6. E. E. Lampard, "The History of Cities in the Economically Advanced Areas," *Economic Development and Cultural Change* 3 (January 1955), p. 89.

7. Thomas M. Stanback and Richard V. Knight, *The Metropolitan Economy* (New York: Columbia University Press, 1970), p. 124.

8. Melvin Mandel, "But I Wouldn't Want to Work There," *New York Times* (November 28, 1971), IV, p. 4.

9. Wolfgang Quante, *The Exodus of Corporate Headquarters from New York City* (New York: Praeger, 1976), pp. 42–45.

10. Quoted in Peter Kihss, "Corporate Services Up in New York Although Big Companies Have Left," *New York Times* (December 14, 1977), B, p. 2.

11. Carter B. Horsley, "Look for a Comeback in '77, Say the Office Market Experts," *New York Times* (March 6, 1977), 8, p. 1; "Suburbia Threatened," *New York Times* (December 3, 1973), p. 38.

12. Gerald Manners, "The Office in Metropolis, an Opportunity for Shaping Metropolitan America," *Economic Geography* 50 (April 1974), pp. 98-99.

13. Edgar M. Hoover and Raymond Vernon, *Anatomy of a Metropolis* (Garden City: Doubleday Anchor, 1962), p. 9.

14. Scott Greer, *Urban Renewal and American Cities* (Indianapolis: Bobbs-Merrill, 1965), pp. 3-34; Lowdon Wingo, Jr., "Urban Renewal: A Strategy for Information and Analysis," *Journal of the American Institute of Planners* 32 (May 1966), pp. 143-154.

15. Harold Kaplan, *Urban Renewal Politics* (New York: Columbia University Press, 1963), pp. 10-38.

16. William G. Grigsby, "A General Strategy for Urban Renewal," in *The Metropolitan Enigma*, ed. James Wilson (Cambridge: Harvard University Press, 1966): p. 654.

17. Martin Anderson, *The Federal Bulldozer* (New York: McGraw-Hill, 1964), pp. 65-67.

18. Cited in Brian Berry, Sandra Parsons, and Rutherford Platt, *The Impact of Urban Renewal on Small Business* (Chicago: Center for Urban Studies, The University of Chicago, 1968), p. 1.

19. Judith Friedman, *The Distribution of U.S. Office and Retail Activity Among and Within Large SMSAs and Changes in Their Distribution, 1948 to 1963* (Ph.D. Dissertation, University of Michigan, 1970), p. 182.

20. Hoover and Vernon, *Anatomy of a Metropolis*, pp. 183-196.

21. Robert Fitch, "Planning New York," in *The Fiscal Crisis of American Cities*, eds. Roger Alcaly and David Mermelstein (New York: Vintage, 1977), pp. 248-249.

22. Larry L. Orr, *Income, Employment, and Urban Residential Location*
23. Eleanore Carruth, "New York Hangs Out the For-Rent Sign," *Fortune* 83 (February 1971), p. 115.

24. Quante, *The Exodus of Corporate Headquarters from New York City*, p. 99.

25. Lawrence A. Alexander, "Downtown and the City," *Downtown Idea Exchange* 20 (December 15, 1973), p. 2.

26. U.S. Bureau of Labor Statistics, *New York in Transition: Population, Jobs, Prices, and Pay in a Decade of Change*, Regional Report no. 34 (New York: Middle Atlantic Regional Office, 1973), p. 19.

27. Michael J. Flax, *Blacks and Whites: An Experiment in Racial Indicators* (Washington: The Urban Institute, 1971), p. 27.

28. Stuart Garfinkle, "Occupations of Women and Black Workers, 1962–1974," *Monthly Labor Review* 98 (November 1975), pp. 25–34.

29. Dale Hiestand, "Minorities," in *New York is Very Much Alive,* ed. Eli Ginzberg (New York: McGraw-Hill, 1973): p. 111.

30. Eugene S. Uyeki, "Occupation and Residence: Cleveland, 1940–1970," *Sociological Focus* 10 (Winter 1977), p. 333.

31. Alexander Ganz and Thomas O'Brien, "The City: Sandbox, Reservation, or Dynamo," *Public Policy* (1973), p. 117.

32. Raymond Vernon, *The Changing Economic Function of the Central City* (New York: Committee for Economic Development, 1959), p. 58.

33. Bennett Harrison, *Urban Economic Development* (Washington: The Urban Institute, 1974), p. 51.

34. Charles Brecher, "The Mismatch Misunderstanding," *New York Affairs* 4 (Winter 1977), p. 8.

35. John J. Kain, "Housing Segregation, Negro Employment, and Metropolitan Decentralization," *Quarterly Journal of Economics* 82 (May 1968), pp. 179–180.

36. Joseph D. Mooney, "Housing Segregation, Negro Employment and Metropolitan Decentralization," *Quarterly Journal of Economics* 83 (May 1969).

37. Stanley Friedlander, *Unemployment in the Urban Core* (New York: Praeger, 1972), pp. 88–89.

38. Stanley Masters, *Black-White Income Differentials* (New York: Academic Press, 1975), p. 88.

39. Bennett Harrison, "Education and Underemployment in the Urban Ghetto in *Problems in Political Economy: An Urban Perspective,* ed. David M. Gordon (Lexington: Heath, 1971), pp. 188–189.

40. Marcia Freedman, *Labor Markets: Segments and Shelters* (Montclair, N.J.: Allanheld, Osmun & Co. Publishers, 1976), pp. 118–19.

41. Harry Braverman, *Labor and Monopoly Capital: The Degradation of Work in the Twentieth Century* (New York: Monthly Review Press, 1974), pp. 293–358.

42. Louise Kapp Howe, "Women Office Workers," *New York Affairs* 4 (Winter 1977), p. 33.

43. Eli Ginzberg, "The Job Problem," *Scientific American* 237 (November 1977), pp. 43–51.

# 2 Ecological, Planning, and Labor Market Perspectives

## Workplace and Residence in the Classical Ecological Models

Each of the three classic models of city development gives a prominent position to the central business district. Ernest Burgess saw the CBD as the focus of commercial, social, and civic life, and as the center of the transportation network.[1] The city expands radially, as the CBD extends into or invades the next circular zone, and each of the zones in turn invades the territory of the next zone. The zone closest to the CBD is called the zone of transition. It is a declining residential area about to be taken over for commercial use by the expanding CBD. The next zone is the workingman's area, and each succeeding zone has a higher status composition. The model has been used often to understand and predict land use development in the city. This pattern of development was evident in many American cities at the time of its formulation in the early part of this century.

Homer Hoyt modified the concentric model with a sector model.[2] The CBD remains the keystone of the expansion process, but similar types of land use originate near the CBD and radiate outward in a star-shaped pattern. Chauncy Harris and Edward Ullman went a step further with a model that showed land use patterns expanding from several discrete nuclei.[3] But even in this model, the central retail district is attached to the point of greatest intracity accessibility, and the financial and governmental centers are either intermingled with or close to the retail shops. Both Hoyt and Ullman have more recent writings in which they reconsider their models.[4] Both point to the changing function of the CBD whereby it is less of a retailing center and more of an office center. Hoyt does not attempt to spell out the implications of this on the competition in the urban land and labor markets. Ullman does show how residential migration leads the way to the suburbs, followed closely by manufacturing and retailing jobs. Service jobs are the slowest to leave (his measure does not include office jobs). Ullman concludes that the CBD will be a "center of much less relative importance than in the past."

In a recent study, John Kasarda investigated the process of ecological expansion of cities.[5] He borrowed the idea of Amos Hawley that expansion involves centripetal movements. The centrifugal movements are the process by which new lands or populations are incorporated into a single city. The centripetal movements develop the center so it can maintain integration and coordination over the expanding complex of relationships. With data from 157 Standard Metropolitan Statistical Areas (SMSAs), he found that the larger the suburban population the greater the degree of organizational functions in the central city. This had a greater effect than size of the central city, age of the SMSA, or distance between metropolitan centers. His indicators of organizational functions were professional, managerial, clerical, financial, insurance, real estate, business and repair services, and public administration jobs. So despite a centrifugal drift of population, he finds this centripetal drift of coordinating and integrating functions. Although he used central city data instead of CBD data, most of these coordinating functions are located in the CBD. So the dominance of the central business district as a control center is increasing as the suburban population spreads. While this does not directly contradict Ullman's statement that the CBD is "a center of much less relative importance" today, it does show that in this one aspect of dominance it is becoming more important.

Much attention has been given to the fact that CBD retail

sales have fallen off. George Sternlieb, in an analysis of many central business districts, says that planning can and should aim at a positive adjustment to a reduced volume of retail trade.[6] Richard Andrews finds that one-third of all CBD retail sales are to the downtown workforce.[7] As more female clerical help is brought into the CBD, it will support retailing. But the CBD will never return to its former prominence as a retail center.

The departure of some economic functions actually has some positive effects in the CBD and the surrounding area. Two examples are the handling of wholesale goods and manufacturing. Both have negative externalities such as pollution, heavy truck traffic, and unsightly facilities. Modern communications, computer inventory control, and transportation allow the offices and salesrooms of these companies to remain downtown, while the goods handling or manufacturing facilities are moved to more economical quarters away from the congested transportation grid and population concentrations. It does mean a loss of jobs in the CBD, especially for semi-skilled and unskilled males. Like retailing, all manufacturing and wholesaling companies will not leave the CBD. Small and specialized companies still seek the economies of scale the CBD offers.[8]

Burgess saw two trends triggering the expansion process in the "zone of transition." On the one hand it was being invaded by business and light manufacturing at its border with the CBD. On the other hand, there is a movement of large numbers of immigrants into the deteriorated housing, and those who made good from earlier immigrant groups are pushed outward.

Neither of these triggering mechanisms appears to have much impact today. The commercial expansion of the CBD is mostly vertical. Manufacturing and wholesaling leapfrog to the suburbs rather than expand into the zone of transition. Raymond Murphy reports on research in nine cities he did in the 1950s which showed that CBD zones of assimilation and discard were generally small.[9] The CBD expanded toward higher residential areas, leaving a zone of discard near railroad or manufacturing areas. Urban Renewal may have reversed this latter trend by clearing large sites in the zones of discard for new office, leisure, or luxury housing uses. But the net amount of

CBD expansion into the zone of transition remains relatively small.

The other triggering mechanism which has lost significance is the inflow of migrant groups. These groups usually ended up in ethnic or racial ghettos in the zone of transition. The last significant people to enter were the blacks, except for Puerto Ricans, Cubans, or Mexicans in some of the border areas. The black migration from the South has slowed substantially. The percent of blacks in the South dropped from 77 percent to 54 percent between 1940 and 1965. Between 1965 and 1973 it only declined to 52 percent.[10] James Quinn finds necessary assumptions in the Burgess model that there is population expansion and a large immigrant population characterized by different degrees of assimilation.[11] Attention must be paid to what happens when these are not present.

George Sternlieb goes so far as to say, "Now that these great migrant flows have been reduced to a comparative trickle, the city has lost its raison d'etre."[12] David Gordon hypothesizes that our economy has adjusted to this decline in migration by inventing mechanisms to keep blacks on the bottom rung of the occupational ladder. The last group in stays at the bottom. It is profitable for business to keep a pool of cheap labor for dirty, tedious, or intermittent jobs, in Gordon's perspective.[13] Similarly, Lester Thurow theorizes about a mutual reinforcement effect of a number of factors including residential and employment ones that combine with racial discrimination to lock the blacks into poverty and into segregated inner-city ghettos.[14] By using a classical residential land use model and by being specific about job types and locations in the city, this study hopes to answer some of the questions raised in Gordon's and Thurow's theory.

Perhaps the zone of transition will merely keep its present trend of thinning out in population. It will undoubtedly keep some of its "hobohemias" as Burgess called them, but a stabilizing pattern may be seen in other parts of the zone. With a combination of less population density, more employment stability, less residential mobility, some return of middle or upper class residents to redeveloped pockets of land, and perhaps some public housing, the nature of the zone in transition could change radically. Murphy notes that highway construction has had a disruptive effect in inner-city neighborhoods, but it also has a positive effect. It has freed many of the streets in the zone of transition from heavy commuter and truck traffic, and thus the areas have become more livable.[15]

Stability of population is a key factor in regenerating neighborhoods. John Kasarda and Morris Janowitz found that community attachment and the development of social bonds are significantly related to length of residence, while they are not related to size and density.[16] If stability is achieved merely through people being trapped by poverty in deteriorating neighborhoods, it will not anchor any rejuvenation. If a stable source of jobs is present nearby, different class groups might seek inner-city residences, and older residents might decide to stay as they move up the class ladder.

Pockets of upper class housing have always been found in the heart of our cities. Luxury apartment buildings often lie in or close to the CBD. Recently, pockets of middle class housing have been emerging in the areas of transition in Washington, Philadelphia, Boston, San Francisco, New Orleans, Denver, Atlanta, Memphis and many other cities. The trend to childless and smaller families gives signs of aiding this trend as there is less need for the spacious suburban home. The energy crisis may further affect the trend by retarding urban sprawl and making long commutation more costly.

The forces of land cost equilibrium may also increase the attractiveness of inner-city renewal or rehabilitation. Maurice Yeates demonstrates that in 1910 land values declined logarithmically with distance from the center of Chicago. By 1960, the logarithmic decline was evident only in a 1.5 mile radius from the center, and land values were increasing toward the periphery.[17] At some point price equilibrium will make lower central city land prices more attractive and competitive.

The connection between the middle class return to the area of transition and white-collar employment in the CBD is evident in recent research findings. S. Gregory Lipton found the most evidence for upward income and educational change in inner-city census tracts (using measures comparing tract medians in SMSAs) in cities whose central business districts were dominated by white-collar employment and which had long commuting distances to the suburbs.[18] Thomas Black studied the renovation of inner-city housing. Most of the occupants of these renovated units were singles or small families and white-collar employees.[19]

Bringing the race factor into the issue further complicates it. A reverse segregation may be occurring as formerly black areas become white areas after rebuilding or renovation. Some poor families, mostly black and Hispanic, have been displaced in Queen Village in Philadelphia, Adams-Morgan in Washington, and similar pockets of inner-city renewal.[20] Perhaps these neighborhoods will emerge as racially integrated neighborhoods. This may depend on the residential choice of blacks in white-collar jobs. Eugene Uyeki, as noted previously, found clerical workers less residentially segregated than any other occupational group.

## The Centrist-Decentrist Controversy

The terms "centrist" and "decentrist" were first used by Catherine Bauer and made popular by Jane Jacobs.[21] The centrists see advantages in clustering many functions and activities into a small urban area. The decentrists want to disperse activities, enterprises, and population as much as possible.

Jane Jacobs traces the most important thread of influence in the decentrist school back to Ebenezer Howard and his Garden City idea. Mumford popularized this view, especially in "The Culture of Cities." The decentrist literature is filled with descriptions of the city as a "monstrosity," "solidified chaos," and the like. They "cry wolf" at the least bit of negative news about the city.

The centrists, on the other hand, claim that the adverse effects of density can be controlled. Jacobs, the most famous popularizer of this view, holds that lively, diverse, and intense cities are the cornerstone of our culture and economic advancement, and that they contain the seeds of their own regeneration. While she is opposed to the large, single function (residential, office, etc.) type of development, she is not opposed to density per se. William Whyte, in his introduction to the New York City Master Plan, provoked a storm of controversy with the statement:

But concentration is the genius of the city, its reason for being, the source of its vitality and its excitement. We believe that the center should be strengthened, not weakened, and we are not afraid of the bogey of high density.[22]

The primary assumption of the New York Master Plan is that the whole city rises or falls on the strength of the core—the "engine" that runs the city.

The Master Plan was not without its opponents, even among the members of the planning commission at that time. Beverly Spatt argued against the "madness" of concentrating more activities in the center. She felt the plan ignored the impact of overcrowding on people.[23] In the mid 1970s, neighborhood activists and politicians from the outer boroughs of the city attacked the Master Plan because it meant, in effect, that Manhattan was getting most of the dollars allocated for capital development. The cry arose to use this money for housing and neighborhood rehabilitation.

Albert Mayer states the case of the neighborhood activists against spending large amounts in the CBD:

How many happy and essential "municipal incidents" could be called into life for even half the cost of a Lincoln Center: How many of our East Harlems, Brownsvilles, Bushwicks, Morrisanias,—and middle-class Elmhursts, too—could reach a new spirited level of community consciousness, community enjoyment. . . ?[24]

Mayor Koch got himself elected in 1977 partly by aligning himself with these neighborhood groups and raising questions about massive new development projects in Manhattan like the Westside Highway. But like most mayors before him, he is spending most of the available development dollars on Manhattan projects like Westway. The priorities may be set more in Washington and in the state capital than at City Hall, but the mayor's hand is always forced when there is a prospect of an income-producing venture in the center of the city. While neighborhood activists may have a just grievance over the unbalanced allocation of funds, they must take into consideration the fact that a mayor has to look beyond the immediate good and interests of neighborhoods. Job supply is not usually an immediate concern of neighborhood leaders.

Beyond the issue in New York City, a similar discussion

takes place in the American planning literature over the question of whether the city needs a "heart." Victor Gruen and Charles Abrams argue that the urban organism, like the human organism, has a heart (the CBD) which is essential to the health of the whole organism. In this view, only the cities with pulsating cores will thrive.[25]

Other planners debate the validity of this analogy. Melvin Webber protests that Los Angeles is a classic case to disprove the heart analogy. He claims that the Los Angeles CBD is simply not very dominant, but this does not hurt the dynamism of the city.[26] Gruen insists that Los Angeles has no soul, that it is a depressing disappointment to the tourist, and that without this soul its social and cultural life is "artificially inseminated and exceedingly sterile." Webber dismisses these comments as myths that derive from "the ideology of metropolitan form." Despite distances, Webber claims that the people of Los Angeles are able to conduct their business face-to-face, perhaps as frequently as New Yorkers. It is not a cultural desert because its cultural activities are not visibly concentrated together. For Webber, the greatest evidence of the vitality of Los Angeles is its tremendous growth.

The argument between the centrists and decentrists can be never-ending without some systematic study. Both sides state their cases in ideological and even emotional terms, and perhaps they overstate their cases. The recent renewal of the Los Angeles CBD apparently contradicts Webber, and shows that the centripetal movement of coordinating functions to the center is taking place even as the population spreads in centrifugal fashion. But the renewal will not produce the thriving center of all metropolitan activities that the centrists say is necessary.

The centrists advocate that CBD renewal should take advantage of the existing infrastructure and economies of scale which the CBD already has. The decentrists claim that this is merely reinforcing the mistakes of the past. Again, this research cannot answer all the questions raised in this controversy, but it will systematically study the impact of the CBD on the economic health of the city, particularly the economic health of the black community.

## Hierarchical and Functional Classifications of Cities

Studies of hierarchical and functional classification of cities shed light on the nature of changes in the CBD. Patterns of growth will vary in different size cities. Richard Knight, for instance, finds that control activities tend to locate in larger cities, while production facilities tend to locate in smaller cities as they become less dependent on the local business infrastructure.[27] Thomas Stanback and Richard Knight find that large cities will lose many functions that spin off to smaller cities, especially consumer services. The large cities will increase the number of jobs in business and recreational services and in certain office specializations in which they have a comparative advantage.[28] At this point, the Stanback and Knight findings parallel those of Armstrong.[29] Medium-sized cities will find some growth in both consumer and business services, the latter especially true in regional centers. Small cities will emphasize consumer services. All these trends affect the shape of the CBD.

Stanback and Knight, Brian Berry, and Robert Beckley propose that different types of cities require different types of infusion of government money to promote economic development. A dollar of government funds for a particular urban project does not necessarily have the same impact in all cities. It is wrong to assume that it is wise to spend money to redevelop every CBD. Stanback and Knight suggest that nodal cities (which have large numbers of jobs in business and consumer services and which export these services to a hinterland) are the cities which profit the most from central business district renewal.[30] The policy implications of this are self-evident.

In conclusion, the impact of changing CBD employment patterns on blacks takes on added importance against the background of the three theoretical perspectives discussed in this chapter. In the classic models, the competition for residential land depends in part on labor market competition and job location. The latter consideration is especially important in determining the future of black inner-city residential areas. In the centrist-decentrist question of the importance of the CBD for the vitality of a city, a key consideration is the lifeblood the CBD pumps into the community through jobs, particularly for inner-city minorities. Finally, as suggestions arise from the functional classifications of cities that public intervention in CBD renewal is very beneficial in nodal cities, this study will show what has happened to black employment in the cities that have had extensive CBD office development.

## Notes

1. Ernest W. Burgess, "The Growth of the City," in *The City*, eds. Robert E. Park, E. W. Burgess, and R. D. McKenzie (Chicago: University of Chicago Press, 1925), pp. 27–62.

2. Homer Hoyt, *The Structure and Growth of Residential Neighborhoods in the United States* (Washington: Federal Housing Administration, 1939).

3. Chauncy Harris and Edward Ullman, "The Nature of Cities," *The Annals of the American Academy of Political and Social Science* 242 (November 1945), pp. 7–17.

4. Homer Hoyt, "Recent Distortions of the Classical Models of Urban Structure," *Land Economics* 40 (May 1964), pp. 199–212; Edward L. Ullman, "The Nature of Cities Reconsidered," *The Regional Science Association Papers* 9 (1962), pp. 7–23.

5. John D. Kasarda, "The Theory of Ecological Expansion: An Empirical Test," *Social Forces* 51 (December 1972), pp. 165–176.

6. George Sternlieb, "The Future of Retailing in the Downtown Core," *Journal of the American Institute of Planners* 29 (February 1963), p. 102.

7. Richard Andrews, *Urban Growth and Development* (New York: Simons-Boardman, 1962).

8. For an extended discussion of this argument, see Donald W. Griffin and Richard E. Preston, "A Restatement of the 'Transition Zone' Concept," *Annals of the Association of American Geographers* 56 (June 1966), pp. 339–350.

9. Raymond E. Murphy, *The Central Business District* (Chicago: Aldine-Atherton, 1972), pp. 62–65.

10. U.S. Bureau of the Census, *Statistical Abstract of the United States*, 96th Edition (Washington; U.S. Government Printing Office, 1975), p. 28.

11. James A. Quinn, *Human Ecology* (New York: Prentice-Hall, 1950), pp. 120–122.

12. George Sternlieb, "The City as Sandbox," *Public Interest* 25 (Fall 1971), p. 16.

13. David M. Gordon, *Theories of Poverty and Underemployment* (Lexington: Lexington Books, 1972), p. 74.

14. Lester Thurow, *Poverty and Discrimination* (Washington, D. C.: The Brookings Institution, 1969).

15. Murphy, *The Central Business District*, p. 133.

16. John Kasarda and Morris Janowitz, "Community Attachment in Mass Society," *American Sociological Review* 39 (June 1974), pp. 328–339.

17. Maurice Yeates, "Some Factors Affecting the Spatial Distribution of Chicago Land Values, 1910–1960," *Economic Geography* 41 (January 1965), pp. 68–69.

18. S. Gregory Lipton, "Evidence of Central City Revival," *Journal of the American Institute of Planners* 43 (April 1977), pp. 139 and 144.

19. Thomas J. Black, "Private-Market Housing Renovation in Central Cities," *Urban Land* 34 (November 1975), p. 7.

20. Robert Reinhold, "Middle-Class Return Displaces Some Urban Poor," *New York Times* (June 5, 1977), pp. 1 and 58.

21. Jane Jacobs, *The Death and Life of Great American Cities* (New York: Vintage Books, 1961), pp. 1–25.

22. New York City Planning Commission, *Plan for New York City, Vol. 1: Critical Issues* (New York, 1969), p. 5.

23. Beverly Moss Spatt, *A Proposal to Change the Structure of City Planning* (New York: Praeger, 1971).

24. Albert Mayer, "The Case for the Sub-City," *Regional Plan News* 76 (December 1964), p. 6.

25. Victor Gruen, *The Heart of Our Cities* (New York: Simon and Schuster, 1964), pp. 83–87; Charles Abrams, "Downtown Decay and Revival," *Journal of the American Institute of Planners* 27 (February 1961), p. 3.

26. Melvin M. Webber, "Order in Diversity: Community Without Propinquity," in *Cities and Space*, ed. Lowdon Wingo, Jr. (Baltimore: Johns Hopkins Press, 1963), pp. 41–46.

27. Richard V. Knight, *Employment Expansion and Metropolitan Trade* (New York: Praeger, 1973), p. 105.

28. Thomas M. Stanback and Richard V. Knight, *The Metropolitan Economy* (New York: Columbia University Press, 1970), pp. 57 and 234.

29. Regina Belz Armstrong, *The Office Industry: Patterns of Growth and Location* (Cambridge: MIT Press, 1972), pp. 23–26.

30. Stanback and Knight, *The Metropolitan Economy*, pp. 250–251; Brian Berry, *Community Development and Regional Growth in the Sixties and Seventies, Vol. 1: Growth Centers in the American Urban System* (Cambridge: Ballinger, 1973), pp. 149 and 158; Robert Beckley, review of *Downtown Improvement Manual* by Emanuel Berk, in *Journal of the American Institute of Planners* 43 (July 1977), p. 313.

# 3   Data Sources and Limitations

## Definition of the Central Business District

The Bureau of the Census, in consultation with local census tract committees, delineates the central business district for SMSAs over 100,000 in population according to the following criteria:

1) It is an area of very high land valuation.

2) It is an area characterized by a high concentration of retail businesses, offices, theaters, hotels, and service businesses.

3) It is an area of high traffic flow.

4) Census tract boundaries are to be used, although in special situations, deviations from this rule are allowed. In practice, most cities use census tract boundaries. All 54 cities sampled in this study have CBDs defined by tracts.[1]

Raymond Murphy registers many objections to this census definition of the CBD. His main objection is that the normal requirement of using census tract boundaries does not allow enough precision. Sometimes residential areas are included with the CBD because the tracts were originally intended to bound residential areas. Sometimes manufacturing areas at the periphery of the CBD are included or excluded arbitrarily depending on which side of the tract boundary they fall.[2] Murphy is a geographer whose main interest is studying the physical shape of the CBD; he has done valuable work on its expansion. He traces this in nine cities on a block-by-block basis. For that purpose, the census definition is not precise enough. Other scientists interested in sales and employment statistics have found the census definition to be adequate.[3] In the present study, the only difficulty encountered was in the measurement of CBD manufacturing employment. That measure was not used because of the problem of arbitrary inclusion or exclusion mentioned above.

## The Sample of Cities

The following characteristics had to be fulfilled before SMSAs were chosen for this study:

1) The SMSA must have CBDs defined by the census. Table 3.1 shows the 54 cities chosen. Some SMSAs, although large enough to have a CBD defined by the census, did not have such an area. Annaheim and Fort Lauderdale were examples of this. In six instances, the SMSAs chosen had two CBDs. These were Greensboro–Winston-Salem–High Point; Los Angeles–Long Beach; Minneapolis–St. Paul; Norfolk–Portsmouth; San Francisco–Oakland; and Tampa–St. Petersburg.

2) The SMSA must have at least 10,000 CBD workers.

3) The SMSA must have at least 400 black CBD workers. This was to insure an adequate number of cases in occupational categories. In fact, Sacramento, with 456 black CBD workers, and Phoenix, with 503, were the only cities in the sample that had less than 840 cases.

4) The SMSA must not have more than 10 percent of central city workers whose place of work is not reported. The average central city nonreporting rate is 7 percent.

Out of all the SMSAs in the country, 54 fulfilled all these requirements. Six cities had to be eliminated (all in Connecticut and New Jersey) because their nonreporting rates for place of work were excessive. A large number of cities were eliminated because there were not enough black CBD workers. New York was eliminated because the census included only the midtown Manhattan area in the CBD, and not the lower Manhattan financial district with its tens of thousands of office

Table 3.1 Standard Metropolitan Statistical Areas Used in Study

| | | |
|---|---|---|
| 1. Akron | 19. Greensboro, Winston-Salem | 37. Omaha |
| 2. Atlanta | 20. Houston | 38. Philadelphia |
| 3. Austin | 21. Indianapolis | 39. Phoenix |
| 4. Baltimore | 22. Jacksonville | 40. Pittsburgh |
| 5. Birmingham | 23. Kansas City | 41. Richmond |
| 6. Boston | 24. Knoxville | 42. Rochester |
| 7. Buffalo | 25. Little Rock | 43. Sacramento |
| 8. Charlotte | 26. Louisville | 44. St. Louis |
| 9. Chicago | 27. Los Angeles | 45. San Antonio |
| 10. Cincinnati | 28. Memphis | 46. San Diego |
| 11. Cleveland | 29. Miami | 47. San Francisco, Oakland |
| 12. Columbus | 30. Milwaukee | 48. Seattle |
| 13. Dallas | 31. Minneapolis, St. Paul | 49. Tampa, St. Petersburg |
| 14. Dayton | 32. Nashville | 50. Toledo |
| 15. Denver | 33. New Orleans | 51. Tulsa |
| 16. Detroit | 34. Newark | 52. Washington |
| 17. Flint | 35. Norfolk, Portsmouth | 53. Youngstown |
| 18. Fort Worth | 36. Oklahoma City | 54. Wichita |

workers. Where possible, tabulations for place of work were taken from printed census data, because those figures were taken from a 15 percent sample. When a more detailed breakdown of occupational categories than the usual nine-category census groupings was needed, data were tabulated from the Bureau of the Census 1970 County Group Public Use Sample. This provides a one-percent sample of census records of individuals in SMSAs larger than 250,000 in population. The Public Use Sample is stored on computer tape.

## The Adequacy of Census Data on Black Employment

Two problems arise in the consideration of whether the census count adequately represents black employment. The first problem is the undercount on those who are never reached by the census. The second is the problem of place of work not being reported. Both problems may introduce a bias in the study. The National Urban League estimates that the undercount for black males averages 8.9 percent, and for black women 4.9 percent.[4] Apparently the less educated, lower status blacks are the ones most often overlooked. This bias simply has to be kept in mind in interpreting the data.

The average nonreporting rate for place of work by blacks is 10 percent. Fortunately the census data allow an enumeration of these nonreporters by occupation.[5] Table 3.2 shows the percentage distributions of occupations for the total black labor force and for the nonreporters in two non-southern and two southern cities. Pittsburgh and Indianapolis were picked to represent the non-southern cities, and Miami and Birmingham were picked to represent the South because the average black wages in each of these cities closely approximated their region's average. These distributions show only a slight skew toward higher percentages of nonreporters in the lower status jobs. The only exception to this would be in the non-southern cities which have a very high percentage of female service workers who do not report place of work. But overall, this bias is not great. Workers were asked to give the address of the place where they started work if they began at a central place each day, or else the place where they worked the most hours the previous week. If an address could not be given, the company name was to be given. In most cases of nonreporting, the census enumerator could not understand or locate the address of the company.

Similar problems exist with persons of Spanish heritage. The most important function of this category in the study was that figures for persons of Spanish heritage, as well as for blacks, were subtracted from totals to get various indicators for whites. In a few instances controls for persons of Spanish heritage were introduced to see if this had any influence on relative black occupational standing, but the effect was always insignificant. The U.S. Census definition of Spanish heritage also varies by region.[6] In the five southwestern states it includes the Spanish-speaking and those with Spanish surnames. In New York, New Jersey, and Pennsylvania, it includes only persons of Puerto Rican birth or parentage. In the 42 other states and the District of Columbia, it includes only the Spanish-speaking.

**The Centrality Index**

An index of relative black residential centrality was prepared for this study. Census tracts were grouped in concentric zones around the CBD, and the percentages of whites and blacks in each zone were determined. The formula first used by Redick

Table 3.2   Occupational Distributions of All Blacks and Blacks
Who Do Not Report Place of Work, 1970

| | Non-South: Pittsburgh and Indianapolis | | South: Miami and Birmingham | |
| | Total Blacks | Nonreporting | Total Blacks | Nonreporting |
| | (percent) | | (percent) | |
|---|---|---|---|---|
| **Male** | | | | |
| Professional | 6.7 | 3.8 | 3.5 | 2.8 |
| Managers | 3.1 | 2.8 | 5.9 | 2.6 |
| Sales | 2.3 | 1.8 | 1.9 | 2.8 |
| Clerical | 9.4 | 9.7 | 5.2 | 4.1 |
| Craftsmen | 14.5 | 15.3 | 13.9 | 15.3 |
| Operatives | 20.6 | 22.1 | 16.7 | 16.8 |
| Transport | 7.8 | 8.3 | 12.9 | 10.9 |
| Laborers | 15.6 | 17.0 | 23.6 | 29.5 |
| Service | 19.9 | 19.2 | 16.3 | 15.2 |
| **Female** | | | | |
| Professional | 9.5 | 4.7 | 10.3 | 7.3 |
| Managers | 1.6 | .1 | 1.1 | .4 |
| Sales | 3.7 | 3.2 | 2.6 | 2.0 |
| Clerical | 25.8 | 13.2 | 13.8 | 10.8 |
| Craftsmen | 1.3 | 1.1 | 1.5 | 1.3 |
| Operatives | 11.8 | 8.6 | 10.6 | 5.8 |
| Transport | .3 | .2 | .6 | .5 |
| Laborers | 1.3 | 1.0 | 1.5 | 2.0 |
| Service | 44.6 | 67.8 | 57.9 | 69.8 |

was employed.[7] It gives a measure of relative centralization of all blacks with respect to whites. An index value of 100 represents the situation in which all blacks live closer to the CBD than all whites. A value of zero indicates that whites and blacks are identically distributed by distance. A value of –100 indicates that all whites live closer to the CBD than all blacks.

This index was prepared for the 48 SMSAs in the sample that had one CBD and for Los Angeles. The Bureau of the Census defines two CBDs for this SMSA, one in Los Angeles and one in Long Beach.[8] But the Los Angeles CBD has 110,362 workers, while the Long Beach CBD has 4,917, of whom 3,382 live in Long Beach itself. For all practical purposes, the Los Angeles SMSA can be treated as if it had one CBD. In the mapping procedure for this index, the city of Long Beach was eliminated.

The only other city where questions arose about the validity of this index was Newark. The Newark SMSA includes many counties that are part of the New York metropolitan area. Many residents of Newark cross the Hudson River to work in the New York CBD. The Newark CBD has 44,470 workers. Of these, 41,827 live in Essex and Union counties, so these counties were the only ones used in the mapping for this index. The labor market of these two counties appeared independent enough from the New York metropolitan labor market to allow for this measure of the centrality of CBD employment in regard to residence. It is still recognized that some workers from Essex and Union counties work in the Manhattan CBD, although they were predominantly the workers in higher status jobs rather than middle or low status jobs.

Forty tracts from each SMSA were sampled to construct this index.[9] In each SMSA, eight vector lines were drawn outward from the center of the CBD at 45 degree angles to each other. In some cities, like Chicago, where the city spreads out only in some directions from the CBD, the angles were reduced, and the eight vector lines were kept. The SMSA was then divided into five concentric circles around the CBD. The size of these zones was determined by taking the average distance from the CBD to the edge of the "urbanized area" on the eight vector lines and then dividing this average distance by five. The "urbanized area" is the populated area of the SMSA, eliminating farm land and unused land. The tracts sampled were those where the vector lines intersected the midpoints of each of the five concentric zones. Only in Austin, Texas, was it necessary to reduce the number of tracts sampled below 40. Because of the small number of tracts in Austin, 24 tracts were chosen where six vector lines intersected the midpoints of four concentric circles.

The sampling of tracts has been used for similar purposes before. Richard Muth sampled 25 tracts at random in cities to find population density gradients.[10] Kent Schwirian tested two methods of choosing sample tracts in Columbus, Ohio.[11] In the first he simply measured mileage distance to the center and laid off eight sectors at 45 degree angles to each other. In contrast to this arbitrary selection of tracts, he also used a more sophisticated ecological scheme. Travel distance times to the center were used, and sectors were laid off which followed the city's rivers, main streets, and rail lines. In testing hypotheses on sector and distance effects on median school years of the population of tracts and the percentage of one-unit dwellings in the tracts, he reached the same conclusion with both the arbitrary and the ecological selection systems. He tentatively concluded that arbitrary schemes are adequate if they are detailed enough. Initially, only four vectors were used in the present study, but an examination of the results showed too much danger of missing concentrations of blacks. In many cities known to the author, this danger was not realized with eight vectors. A greater problem for sampling is the variation in the size of census tracts, particularly in southern cities. If an unusually large or small tract is chosen, it can distort the percentages for that zone.

The cumulative percentages of blacks and whites for each of the five zones beginning with the innermost zone were prepared. Redick's formula is then applied:[12]

Index of Centralization $= \Sigma \ X_{i=1} \ Y_i \ - \ \Sigma \ Y_{i=1} \ X_i$

In this formula, $X_{i-1} \ Y_i$ is the cumulative percentage for whites in a zone ($Y_i$) multiplied by the cumulative percentage of blacks in the next zone closer to the CBD ($X_{i-1}$). In a similar way, $Y_{i-1} \ X_i$ is the cumulative percentage of blacks in a zone multiplied by the cumulative percentage of whites in the next zone closer to the center.

In Tables 3.3 and 3.4 the cities in the non-South and South are ranked by their scores on the Index of Centralization. The southern region includes cities in Virginia, West Virginia, North Carolina, South Carolina, Georgia, Florida, Kentucky, Tennessee, Mississippi, Alabama, Arkansas, Louisiana, Oklahoma, and Texas.

The Sorensen, Taeuber, Hollingsworth Index of Residential Segregation is also presented in Tables 3.3 and 3.4.[13] If blacks and whites were distributed identically among city blocks, this index would have a value of zero. This would mean there would be the same percentage of blacks and whites on each block as the percentage of blacks and whites in the whole SMSA. If the races were distributed so that no block would have white and black households, the index would have a value of

Table 3.3    Black Centralization and Residential Segregation Indexes:
32 Non-Southern Cities, 1970

|  | Black Centralization Index | Residential Segregation Index |
|---|---|---|
| Sacramento | 22.3 | 71.1 |
| Pittsburgh | 39.0 | 85.9 |
| Omaha | 39.3 | 89.6 |
| Phoenix | 41.8 | N.A. |
| Wichita | 43.6 | 93.0 |
| Dayton | 44.9 | 91.1 |
| Philadelphia | 50.2 | 84.4 |
| Cincinnati | 50.9 | 84.2 |
| Los Angeles | 51.0 | 90.5 |
| Flint | 52.4 | 82.9 |
| Denver | 52.6 | 88.9 |
| Boston | 54.0 | 84.3 |
| Chicago | 54.7 | 93.0 |
| Baltimore | 55.8 | 89.4 |
| Youngstown | 57.6 | 75.9 |
| San Diego | 57.9 | 85.6 |
| Toledo | 64.2 | 89.1 |
| Columbus | 65.0 | 86.2 |
| Newark | 68.5 | 76.4 |
| Washington | 68.7 | 78.8 |
| Kansas City | 71.9 | 90.5 |
| Akron | 73.8 | 82.5 |
| Rochester | 76.6 | 76.5 |
| Cleveland | 78.0 | 90.1 |
| St. Louis | 78.2 | 90.1 |
| Buffalo | 78.3 | 87.3 |
| Indianapolis | 79.0 | 89.6 |
| Milwaukee | 79.2 | 88.0 |
| Seattle | 79.7 | 82.2 |
| Detroit | 81.8 | 82.1 |
| Minneapolis | N.A. | 80.4 |
| San Francisco | N.A. | 75.0 |

N.A. = Not Available

Source:    Index of Block Residential Segregation for Whites and Negroes taken from
Annemette Sorenson, Karl Taeuber, and Leslie Hollingsworth, *Studies in Racial
Segregation,* No. 1. Madison, Wisconsin: Institute for Research on Poverty,
University of Wisconsin, 1974 (used with permission of authors).

100. The index also indicates the percentage of either the white
or black households that would have to move to blocks
containing the other group to attain an unsegregated
distribution.

Table 3.4    Black Centralization and Residential Segregation Indexes:
22 Southern Cities, 1970

|  | Black Centralization Index | Residential Segregation Index |
|---|---|---|
| Knoxville | 17.5 | 92.2 |
| San Antonio | 33.3 | 89.7 |
| Miami | 38.4 | 92.0 |
| Little Rock | 40.3 | 90.6 |
| Houston | 42.1 | 92.7 |
| Tulsa | 43.3 | 94.5 |
| Austin | 46.2 | 90.2 |
| Jacksonville | 46.9 | 94.3 |
| Louisville | 48.7 | 89.7 |
| Memphis | 52.7 | 92.4 |
| Birmingham | 52.7 | 91.8 |
| Dallas | 54.7 | 95.9 |
| Oklahoma City | 55.3 | 95.6 |
| Fort Worth | 55.3 | 95.4 |
| Charlotte | 59.2 | 93.7 |
| New Orleans | 60.1 | 83.9 |
| Atlanta | 62.5 | 91.9 |
| Richmond | 71.6 | 91.4 |
| Nashville | 74.5 | 90.3 |
| Norfolk | N.A. | 93.5 |
| Greensboro | N.A. | 03.0 |
| Tampa | N.A. | 92.0 |

N.A. = Not Available

Source:    Index of Block Residential Segregation for Whites and Negroes taken from
Annemette Sorenson, Karl Taeuber, and Leslie Hollingsworth, *Studies in
Racial Segregation,* No. 1. Madison, Wisconsin: Institute for Research on
Poverty, University of Wisconsin, 1974 (used with permission of authors).

## The Definition of Indexes

The relative occupational status of black workers is measured
in two ways. The first is an Index of Occupational Dissimilarity between the nine census occupational categories for
white and black CBD workers by sex. This index indicates the
percentage of blacks who would have to switch jobs so that the
distribution of jobs across the nine census categories of occupations would be the same for blacks and whites. An index value
of zero would indicate an equal distribution of jobs among the
races, while a value of 100 would indicate a total segregation

where blacks and whites were never found in the same job categories.

The second measure of the relative occupational status of black workers is the Relative Minority Income Ratio. This is the ratio of average black income to average white income of CBD workers. Both of these indicators were tabulated from census material for each sex and sometimes for different age groups in each city.[14]

In order to measure the participation level of blacks in certain CBD occupational categories, a Black Employment Equality Index is used. This is a ratio of the percentage of jobs in a particular occupation held by blacks to the percentage of all jobs in the CBD that are held by blacks. If the index is less than 1.00, blacks are underrepresented in that occupation. If the index score is greater than 1.00, blacks are overrepresented in that category compared to whites.

The Office Concentration Index measures the percentage of office jobs in the CBD labor force. This is basically the census category "clerical" with nonoffice jobs such as cashier and mailman excluded. This was calculated from the computer tapes of the Public Use Sample of the Bureau of the Census.

## Notes

1. U.S. Bureau of the Census, *Census of Population; Detailed Characteristics*, Final Report PC (1)-D: Appendix B.

2. Raymond E. Murphy, *The Central Business District* (Chicago: Aldine-Atherton, 1972), pp. 109–111.

3. Edgar M. Horwood and Ronald R. Boyce, *Studies of the Central Business District and Urban Freeway Development* (Seattle: University of Washington Press, 1959); Ronald R. Boyce and W. A. V. Clark, "Selected Spatial Variables and Central Business District Sales," *Proceedings of the Regional Science Association* 11: pp. 167–193; Judith Lynn Johnson Friedman, "The Distribution of U.S. Office and Retail Activity Among and Within Large SMSAs and Changes in Their Distribution, 1948 to 1963," (Ph.D. Dissertation, University of Michigan, 1970).

4. Joan R. Harris, "Minorities and Women," *ASA Footnotes* 1 (November 1973), p. 6.

5. U.S. Bureau of the Census, *Census of Population; 1970 Detailed Characteristics*, Table 190.

6. *Ibid.*, Appendix B.

7. Richard W. Redick, "Population Growth and Distribution in Central Cities, 1940–1950," *American Sociological Review* 21 (February 1956), pp. 38–43.

8. U.S. Bureau of the Census, *Census of Population and Housing; 1970 Census Tracts,* Final Report PHC (1), Table P-2.

9. *Ibid.,* Table P-1.

10. Richard Muth, *Cities and Housing* (Chicago: University of Chicago Press, 1969), p. 141.

11. Kent P. Schwirian, "Some Recent Trends and Methodological Problems in Urban Ecological Research," in *Comparative Urban Structure,* ed. Kent P. Schwirian (Lexington: D. C. Heath, 1974), pp. 25–27.

12. Redick, *op. cit.,* p. 40.

13. Annemette Sorensen, Karl E. Taeuber, and Leslie J. Hollingsworth, *Indexes of Racial Residential Segregation for 109 Cities in the United States, 1940 to 1970* (Madison: University of Wisconsin, Institute for Research on Poverty, 1974).

14. U.S. Bureau of the Census, *Census of Population; 1970 Detailed Characteristics,* Table 190.

# 4    The Mismatch Hypothesis Qualified

## The Mismatch Hypothesis

Before specific information is presented on CBD employment, an overall look at the distribution of workplace and residence in the metropolis will be presented. The framework for this analysis will be taken from the research on the mismatch hypothesis. Even though the conceptualization of the mismatch hypothesis falls short of an adequate explanation of the urban labor market, the research offers a systematic process for relating the workplace and residence of the worker.

The statistics on changing job locations and commutation to suburban jobs justify close examination of the mismatch hypothesis. David Birch pointed to an increase in the percentage of central city residents commuting to suburban jobs in 120 large cities between 1960 and 1970 (an increase from 10 percent to 20 percent in mid-size SMSAs and from 9 percent to 14 percent in large SMSAs).[1] Brian Berry and John Kasarda found that 49 percent of blacks working in the suburbs in 1970 commuted from the central city, and that 14.8 percent of black workers residing in the central city commuted to the suburbs or beyond the SMSA limits.[2] Edward Kalachek and John Goering's study of St. Louis revealed greater outward reverse commuting for blue-collar than for white-collar workers.[3] All of these findings lend credence to the mismatch hypothesis.

Men feel the negative impact of the suburbanization of jobs more than women. Neil Gold highlighted the fact that in the 1960s, male employment in the central cities dropped by 2 percent while female employment increased by 17.5 percent.[4] Is this changing sex composition a characteristic of the whole labor market, or is it the result of changing distributions of job locations in the city? The framework of the conceptualization and measurement ratios utilized by researchers on the mismatch hypothesis can give an answer to this question.

The publicity given to industrial plants relocating to suburbs, to reverse bus transportation experiments in a dozen cities,[5] and to the accusations against suburbs for zoning out the low-skilled who work there, point to the need for more precise information on the relation between workplace and residence.

## Previous Evaluations

The aspect of the mismatch theory that has caused the most interest, and which has been the basis for policy, is the separation between the residences of the low-skilled workers in the central city and the available jobs for them in the suburbs. Most of the formal research on the question, however, has found the mismatch hypothesis oversimplified.

Charlotte Fremon claimed the mismatch hypothesis was disproven by her data from eight large American cities for the years 1965 through 1967. She found that although the job growth rate in central cities was not as high as that in the suburbs, the central city growth rate was still substantial. The central city growth was not noticeably skewed in favor of the high-skilled white-collar jobs, as many feared.[6] But despite this growth of jobs in all skill categories in the central city, Fremon uncovered some disturbing factors. Unemployment rates remained high in the central city, especially among blacks. The rate of growth of population in the central cities was greater than the rate of growth of employment among central city residents, despite the growing availability of jobs there.[7] Fremon does not offer workplace and residence statistics by race, but merely cites the racial unemployment rates at that time.

Other researchers have noted this increased supply of jobs in the central city along with the inability of the residents to take advantage of them. John Kain discovered an offsetting trend to the employment dispersal to the suburbs in the Chicago area in the 1950s, in that the central city labor market demand remained strong. Despite this, he found black employment worsening.[8] Bennett Harrison cited various researchers who found data indicating reduced competition for jobs in the central city (an increase in the ratio of jobs to central city residents), at the same time the employment of central city residents was falling.[9] The apparent contradiction suggests that suburbanites might still compete for semi-skilled and low-skilled jobs in the central city despite the distance, or that blacks can not break into any part of the urban labor market easily.

## Black Patterns of Workplace and Residence Different From White Patterns

To analyze the mismatch hypothesis, data from 27 cities out of the 54 cities in the whole sample will be used. The 27 cities were those for which land annexed to the central city between 1960 and 1970 had less than 1 percent of the 1970 population. Data are available from the 1960 census giving the number of workers by occupational category for central cities, and for fringe areas (suburban areas beyond the city line). The workplace data is cross-tabulated with residence—central city or fringe. A correction factor was included with the 1960 data to make it comparable with 1970 data. The 1960 data gave tabulations for workers 14 and above. The 1970 data gave tabulations for workers 16 and above. The 1960 census gave information which allowed estimation of the numbers of 14- and 15-year-old workers in skill categories in urban places.[10] These estimated numbers were subtracted from the totals for workers in the 1960 data.

The 1970 census added new categories which allows a breakdown of skill categories for jobs in the CBD, the remainder of the central city, and the fringe. It also allows a breakdown for white, black, and Hispanic workers. Ten of the 27 cities had sufficient Hispanic workers to give detailed occupational breakdowns.[11] There are not enough data on the Hispanics to give an elaborate analysis of their workplace and residence patterns. The statistics for "whites" have the Hispanic numbers subtracted from them.

The definitions of the various skill categories have been taken from Charlotte Fremon.[12] The high-skilled category includes officials and managers, professionals and technical workers. The semi-skilled category includes sales workers, office and clerical workers, craftsmen, and operatives. The low-skilled category includes laborers and service workers. It is difficult to group categories which are already heterogeneous, but for the purpose of getting a general picture of the distribution of jobs in the city, this categorization appears adequate. Fremon found that if craftsmen were considered high-skilled and technicians semi-skilled, the results of the analysis were changed very little.

First the composite data for all workers will be presented. Then the data for blacks, whites, and Hispanics will be given. Table 4.1 shows that there has been a substantial drop in the percentage of SMSA jobs located in the city, particularly in semi-skilled and low-skilled categories. More than 50 percent of the jobs in most skill categories are now in the suburbs, excepting the high-skilled jobs for men and the semi-skilled jobs for women. These latter categories contain most of the office workers of the CBD.

Table 4.2 tells the story of the suburbanization of jobs even more dramatically with the actual number of jobs gained or lost in the central city between 1960 and 1970. The number of semi-skilled jobs for men in the central city plunged by 17.2 percent. The number of low-skilled jobs dropped for both men and women. Fremon did not disaggregate the data by sex, and so her totals masked the severe drop in the semi-skilled category for men.

This evidence supports the "mismatch hypothesis," insofar as the mismatch means a flight of semi-skilled and low-skilled jobs from the central city. It refutes the position of Charlotte Fremon who claimed that the growth in central city jobs was not noticeably skewed in favor of high-skilled white collar jobs,

27 Metropolitan Areas
(Tables 4.1 through 4.8)

| | | |
|---|---|---|
| Akron | Detroit* | Norfolk, Portsmouth |
| Atlanta | Flint | Philadelphia* |
| Baltimore | Los Angeles* | Pittsburgh |
| Birmingham | Miami* | Rochester |
| Boston* | Milwaukee | St. Louis |
| Buffalo | Minneapolis, St. Paul | San Francisco, Oakland* |
| Chicago* | Nashville | Seattle |
| Cincinnati | New Orleans* | Washington* |
| Cleveland | Newark* | Youngstown |

*The data for Hispanics in Table 4.7 were taken from these ten cities.

Table 4.1    Percent of Metropolitan Employment in Central City
by Skill Category, 1960-1970 (27 cities)

| | High-skilled | Semi-skilled | Low-skilled |
|---|---|---|---|
| Male | | | |
| 1960[a] | 60.2 | 50.6 | 59.9 |
| 1970 | 52.1 | 48.5 | 49.0 |
| Female | | | |
| 1960[a] | 56.3 | 04.0 | 50.8 |
| 1970 | 48.7 | 52.0 | 46.6 |

as the "mismatch" theorists feared. The evidence shows surprising differences with the evidence presented by Fremon. Fremon used Equal Employment Opportunity Commission data which had information only from private employers who had more than 100 employees (about 50 percent of the total labor force.) Fremon had data for only a two-year period, 1965–1967, which was a period of economic expansion. She only had data for eight cities. In contrast, this study had data for 27 cities for a 10-year period, and it covered almost 100 percent of the labor force in each city. The data base apparently explains the discrepancies, but the present study presents much more solid evidence for the mismatch hypothesis. Later in the chapter, the data will be disaggregated by race.

Table 4.2    Spatial Distribution of Employment Change
by Skill Category, 1960-1970 (27 cities)

| | Number of Jobs | | |
| | High-skilled | Semi-skilled | Low-skilled |
|---|---|---|---|
| **Male** | | | |
| Central City | | | |
| 1960 | 1,677,006 | 4,022,248 | 926,786 |
| 1970 | 1,766,257 | 3,329,478 | 866,233 |
| Change | 89,251 | -692,770 | -60,553 |
| | 5.3% | -17.2% | -6.5% |
| Suburbs | | | |
| 1960 | 1,110,749 | 2,274,084 | 620,341 |
| 1970 | 1,618,072 | 3,534,126 | 901,684 |
| Change | 510,593 | 810,042 | 281,343 |
| | 46.1% | 29.7% | 45.4% |
| **Female** | | | |
| Central City | | | |
| 1960 | 554,712 | 2,309,225 | 653,743 |
| 1970 | 722,041 | 2,450,124 | 633,295 |
| Change | 167,329 | 140,899 | -20,448 |
| | 30.2% | 6.1% | -3.1% |
| Suburbs | | | |
| 1960 | 431,186 | 1,254,335 | 487,789 |
| 1970 | 760,031 | 2,259,501 | 726,689 |
| Change | 328,845 | 1,005,166 | 238,900 |
| | 76.3% | 80.1% | 48.9% |

The loss of semi-skilled and low-skilled jobs for men is bound to have a profound impact. In addition to the problem of the flight of jobs from the central city, there is another problem. There is little net gain in semi-skilled jobs for men even after suburban growth is taken into account. In the 27 metropolitan areas studied, the central cities lost 692,000 of these jobs, while the suburbs gained 810,000. The gain hardly cancelled the loss. This is part of a national trend. The middle steps on the American social status ladder for men are decreasing as a percentage of jobs available. The drop in central city jobs that many attribute almost exclusively to a shift in job location may be due in large part to a disappearance of these jobs from the labor market.

**Table 4.3  Spatial Distribution of Employment in City by Skill Category, 1970 (27 cities)**

| Place of Work | High-skilled | Percent | Semi-skilled | Percent | Low-skilled | Percent |
|---|---|---|---|---|---|---|
| Male |  |  |  |  |  |  |
| CBD | 394,044 | 11.6 | 396,888 | 5.8 | 110,395 | 6.2 |
| Remainder of Central City | 1,372,213 | 40.5 | 2,932,590 | 42.7 | 755,838 | 42.8 |
| Fringe | 1,618,072 | 47.9 | 3,534,126 | 51.5 | 901,684 | 51.0 |
| Total |  | 100.0 |  | 100.0 |  | 100.0 |
| Female |  |  |  |  |  |  |
| CBD | 106,364 | 7.2 | 580,337 | 12.3 | 69,310 | 5.1 |
| Remainder of Central City | 615,677 | 41.5 | 1,869,787 | 39.7 | 563,985 | 41.5 |
| Fringe | 760,031 | 51.3 | 2,259,501 | 48.0 | 726,689 | 53.4 |
| Total |  | 100.0 |  | 100.0 |  | 100.0 |

Table 4.4   Ratio of Central City Jobs to Central City Residents Employed in Each Skill Category, 1960-1970 (27 cities)

|  | High-skilled | Semi-skilled | Low-skilled |
|---|---|---|---|
| Male |  |  |  |
| 1960 | 1.71 | 1.30 | 1.05 |
| 1970 | 1.66 | 1.28 | 1.03 |
| Female |  |  |  |
| 1960 | 1.18 | 1.27 | 1.02 |
| 1970 | 1.23 | 1.25 | .97 |

For women in the central city, the problem is not as critical. But even for women, the prime growth areas for semi-skilled and low-skilled jobs have been in the suburbs. The suburbs added a million semi-skilled jobs for women while the central city gained only 140,000.

The data for CBD workers in 1970 is added in Table 4.3. The two groups for which the CBD provides a significant amount of jobs are high-skilled men (11.6 percent) and semi-skilled women (12.3 percent.)

Table 4.4 shows the ratio of the number of jobs in each skill category in the central city to the number of central city residents with those skills. When the value of the ratio is greater than 1.0, it means there are more jobs in the central city than there are central city residents with those skills, and that suburbanites fill the excess of jobs. The ratio for high-skilled males (1.66 in 1970) shows that many men have to be brought in from the suburbs to fill these positions. For low-skilled men the ratio drops almost to 1.0, and it drops below 1.0 for low-skilled women. There are not enough jobs in the central city to employ all its low-skilled female residents who work.

Table 4.4, however, reveals one interesting and unexpected finding. The ratios show amazing stability between 1960 and 1970 despite the varying rates of increase or decrease in jobs by skill category over the decade. The same stability was found in comparing the census data for all SMSAs in 1960 and 1970. There is a close relation between the labor market and residential markets in the city. Labor market changes can be used to

Table 4.5   Spatial Distribution of Black Employment in City by Skill Category, 1970 (27 cities)

| Place of Work | High-skilled | Percent | Semi-skilled | Percent | Low-skilled | Percent |
|---|---|---|---|---|---|---|
| Male | | | | | | |
| CBD | 12,685 | 9 4 | 46,793 | 6.2 | 30,701 | 8.0 |
| Remainder of Central City | 84,356 | 62 4 | 446,519 | 59.3 | 224,752 | 58.8 |
| Fringe | 38,096 | 28 2 | 259,826 | 34.5 | 126,703 | 33.2 |
| Total | | 100.0 | | 100.0 | | 100.0 |
| Female | | | | | | |
| CBD | 10,975 | 7.6 | 77,539 | 15.2 | 23,269 | 6.0 |
| Remainder of Central City | 99,121 | 68.3 | 307,952 | 60.5 | 228,290 | 59.0 |
| Fringe | 35,084 | 24.2 | 123,806 | 24.3 | 136,073 | 35.1 |
| Total | | 100.1 | | 100.0 | | 100.1 |

predict the type of people who migrate from central city to suburb. In order to keep these ratios so constant, there must have been an especially large shift by male semi-skilled and low-skilled workers from residences in the central city to the suburbs.

Fremon, Kain, and Harrison all found data which indicated that job competition in the central city had not worsened substantially despite the suburbanization of jobs. Insofar as the ratio between central city jobs and central city residents remained unchanged from 1960 to 1970, it appears that the supply did not outrun the demand. It remains to be seen how blacks shared in the movement of jobs and residences.

Tables 4.5, 4.6, and 4.7 present place of work data for blacks, whites and Hispanics respectively. In CBD jobs held by men, there are higher percentages of metropolitan area blacks employed in the semi-skilled and low-skilled jobs than of whites. The exception is high-skilled jobs, where the percentage of metropolitan area whites employed in the CBD exceeds that of blacks. In all skill categories among women, there are higher percentages of metropolitan area blacks employed in the CBD than of whites. The two skill categories which have relatively large percentages of the white metropolitan labor force employed are high-skilled male and semi-skilled female. The whites competed strongly in these categories which include most of the office jobs. But the office expansion of the CBD has been large enough to employ high percentages of both black and white women.

What emerges most clearly from these tables is the difference between white and black distributions in the "remainder of the central city" areas. In all of the skill categories, about 60 percent of the metropolitan area blacks are employed in the remainder. Whites in the various skill categories have an average of less than 40 percent working in central cities outside the CBD. The blacks are very dependent on these jobs, many of which are in their own neighborhoods. John Kain found a very large overrepresentation of non-white employees in ghetto workplace zones in Chicago.[13] While the data in this study cannot be broken down for areas as small as the neighborhoods that Kain examined, it is safe to infer that ghetto neighborhoods provide many of the jobs for blacks.

The main job location for better than 50 percent of whites

Table 4.6 Spatial Distribution of White Employment in City by Skill Category, 1970 (27 cities)

| Place of Work | High-skilled | Percent | Semi-skilled | Percent | Low-skilled | Percent |
|---|---|---|---|---|---|---|
| Male | | | | | | |
| CBD | 372,346 | 11.8 | 335,616 | 5.8 | 74,334 | 5.8 |
| Remainder of Central City | 1,250,191 | 39.5 | 2,334,632 | 40.4 | 485,436 | 37.9 |
| Fringe | 1,542,635 | 48.7 | 3,112,015 | 53.8 | 722,190 | 56.3 |
| Total | | 100.0 | | 100.0 | | 100.0 |
| Female | | | | | | |
| CBD | 92,764 | 7.1 | 477,026 | 12.0 | 43,904 | 4.8 |
| Remainder of Central City | 501,364 | 38.4 | 1,467,487 | 36.8 | 312,858 | 34.0 |
| Fringe | 711,058 | 54.5 | 2,045,870 | 51.3 | 562,670 | 61.2 |
| Total | | 100.0 | | 100.1 | | 100.0 |

**Table 4.7 Spatial Distribution of Hispanic Employment in City by Skill Category, 1970 (10 cities)**

| Place of Work | High-skilled | Percent | Semi-skilled | Percent | Low-skilled | Percent |
|---|---|---|---|---|---|---|
| Male | | | | | | |
| CBD | 9,013 | 10.7 | 14,479 | 4.4 | 5,360 | 5.2 |
| Remainder of Central City | 37,666 | 44.8 | 151,439 | 46.1 | 45,650 | 44.0 |
| Fringe | 37,341 | 44.4 | 162,285 | 49.4 | 52,791 | 50.9 |
| Total | | 99.9 | | 99.9 | | 100.1 |
| Female | | | | | | |
| CBD | 2,625 | 8.3 | 25,772 | 12.3 | 2,137 | 4.0 |
| Remainder of Central City | 15,192 | 47.9 | 94,348 | 44.9 | 22,837 | 43.2 |
| Fringe | 13,889 | 43.8 | 89,825 | 42.8 | 27,946 | 52.8 |
| Total | | 100.0 | | 100.0 | | 100.0 |

was the suburbs, except in the case of the high-skilled males. Even the high-skilled males fill just under 50 percent (48.7 percent). The percentages of metropolitan area blacks who worked in the suburbs varied between 24 percent and 35 percent in the different skill categories.

Table 4.8 shows the ratio of the number of central city jobs held by each race in each skill category to the number of central city residents of each race in the particular skill category. The number .79, for instance, indicates that a maximum of 79 percent of the male, black, central city residents in the high-skilled category have jobs in the central city. The actual percentage is less, since some suburban blacks hold central city jobs. The ratios are remarkably low in all of the skill categories for black men, and they are only slightly higher for women. Of the 1,131, 350 black male workers residing in the central cities of these 27 metropolitan areas, at least 285,000 had to get jobs in the suburbs. Of the 887,200 black women, at least 140,000 had to find employment in the suburbs. It may be that blacks prefer to live in the city even when they work in the suburbs. Perhaps they are allowed to work in the suburbs, but prevented by discrimination from living there. Whatever the reason, the fact is clear that many more blacks work in the suburbs than live in the suburbs, and that this is true in all skill categories for both sexes.

The mismatch hypothesis postulates that the semi-skilled and low-skilled jobs fleeing the central city are causing the mismatch for blacks. But the finding is that the blacks have difficulty in getting central city jobs in any skill category. The

Table 4.8    Ratio of Central City Jobs to Central City Residents Employed in Each Skill Category among Blacks and Whites, 1970 (27 cities)

|  | High-skilled | Semi-skilled | Low-skilled |
|---|---|---|---|
| Male |  |  |  |
| White | 1.76 | 1.47 | 1.17 |
| Black | .79 | .72 | .79 |
| Female |  |  |  |
| White | 1.31 | 1.36 | 1.07 |
| Black | .92 | .83 | .83 |

concept of skill mismatch does not adequately explain the situation. Blacks have a difficult time fitting into the older blue-collar jobs of the central city, in part because whites have held the jobs for years, in part because the number of central city blue-collar jobs has been contracting, and in part due to discrimination or lack of skill. The blacks have also had trouble fitting into the expanding white-collar sector. Whites offer strong competition for these central city jobs even though they live farther from them than the blacks.

## The Metropolitan Labor Market—Context of the CBD Labor Market

The CBD provided 7 percent of the jobs held by the black male workforce in the 27 cities, and 10.7 percent of the jobs for the female black workforce in 1970. While the U.S. Census did not provide CBD workforce statistics for 1960, it is obvious that the CBD had a sizeable share of the semi-skilled and low-skilled job loss of the central cities in the 1960s. The only skill categories which registered a gain in the central cities were the high-skilled male and semi-skilled female jobs. A significant amount of this growth was in the offices of the CBD. Blacks registered some gains in these categories, but encountered stiff competition from whites for them.

So far, the picture of black employment has been painted in broad strokes, because the employment categories were so broad. The corporation president and the school teacher were counted equally in the high-skilled category. The executive secretary and the hardware store salesperson were counted equally in the semi-skilled category. Subsequent chapters will give more detailed decriptions of the jobs held by blacks and whites in the CBD, and descriptions of the types of blacks holding these jobs. It is unrealistic to expect older blacks to fit into many of these jobs, so the younger blacks will be considered carefully.

## Conclusions

1) There has been a substantial drop in the percentage of SMSA jobs located in the central city between 1960 and 1970, especially in the semi-skilled and low-skilled categories.

2) There has been a drop in the absolute numbers of low-skilled jobs for both sexes, and of semi-skilled jobs for men in the central city. Part of this is due to changing job locations, and part is due to the disappearance of these jobs from the economy.

3) Semi-skilled jobs for women (mostly sales and office work) increased substantially, providing many new jobs both in central cities and suburbs.

4) Whites from the suburbs commute in disproportionate numbers to take high-skilled jobs for men and semi-skilled jobs for women in the CBD. The expansion of the number of semi-skilled jobs for women opened opportunities for women of both races.

5) The ratio of central city jobs in each skill category to central city residents with each of these skills remained amazingly constant between 1960 and 1970. These ratios could only have been kept constant by the movement of a large number of white workers to suburban homes to be closer to the semi-skilled and low-skilled jobs which had moved there.

6) A large number of central city blacks, particularly men, took jobs in the suburbs, but few moved their residences there. Whether it be through discrimination or the self-choice of blacks, it is clear that residential areas remain more segregated than the workplace.

## Notes

1. David L. Birch, "From Suburb to Urban Place," *Annals of the American Academy of Political and Social Science* 422 (November 1975), p. 29.

2. Brian J. L. Berry and John D. Kasarda, *Contemporary Urban Ecology* (New York: Macmillan, 1977), pp. 242-243.

3. Edward Kalachek and John Goering, eds., *Transportation and Central City Unemployment* (St. Louis: Institute for Urban and Regional Studies, 1970), Tables A-3 and A-4.

4. Neil N. Gold, "The Mismatch of Jobs and Low-Income People in Metropolitan Areas and Its Implications for the Central City Poor," in *United States Commission on Population Growth and the American Future, vol. V: Population Distribution and Policy* (Washington: U.S. Government Printing Office, 1972), p. 461.

5. John M. Goering and Edward M. Kalachek, "Public Transportation and Black Unemployment," *Society* 10 (July-August 1973), pp. 39-42.

6. Charlotte Fremon, *The Occupational Patterns in Urban Employment Change, 1965-1967* (Washington: The Urban Institute, 1970), pp. 1-2.

7. *Ibid.*, pp. 15-17.

8. John T. Kain, "Housing Segregation, Negro Employment, and Metropolitan Decentralization," *Quarterly Journal of Economics* 82 (May 1968), pp. 194-196.

9. Bennett Harrison, *Urban Economic Development* (Washington: The Urban Institute, 1974), pp. 42-51.

10. U.S. Bureau of the Census, *Census of Population, 1960; Detailed Characteristics*, Tables 131, 196, 204.

11. U.S. Bureau of the Census, *Census of Population, 1970; Detailed Characteristics*, Table 190.

12. Fremon, *op. cit.*, p. 22.

13. Kain, *op. cit.*, p. 186.

# 5   CBD Jobs for Blacks and Whites

## Office Jobs in the CBD

The 1970 census allows a close examination of employment patterns in the CBD. The first part of this chapter will examine office and office-related jobs. The second part will examine detailed occupational breakdowns of all CBD workers.

In the categorizations that appear in this chapter, "high level clerical jobs" includes office job categories that have an average salary above the mean for female clerical workers. This category includes computer and peripheral equipment operators, key punch operators, payroll and timekeeping clerks, legal, medical and other specialized secretaries, and stenographers. "Low level clerical jobs" refers to those classifications of office jobs that have an average salary below the mean for female clerical workers. Some men hold these jobs, but for the sake of definition, this category is defined in relation to the salaries of women who hold these positions. This category includes bank tellers, billing clerks, bookkeepers, clerical assistants, clerical supervisors, bill collectors, enumerators, estimators and investigators, file clerks, library attendants and assistants, bookkeeping and billing machine operators, calculating machine operators, duplicating machine operators, tabulating and office machine operators, proofreaders, re-

ceptionists, statistical clerks, telegraph and telephone operators, typists, and other miscellaneous office workers.

"Managerial and professional jobs" include all professional, technical, managerial, and administrative jobs as defined by
the Bureau of the Census. In the first part of this chapter where
office employment is being examined, employees in education
and health services are excluded. "Office-associated jobs"
include mail handlers, messengers, postal clerks, electrotypers,
stereotypers, air conditioning and heating repairmen, data
processing and office machine repairmen, parking attendants,
janitorial services, food services, private protection services,
and various personal services.

Table 5.1 shows the distribution of office and office-related
jobs in CBDs by race and sex in all 54 cities of the sample. At the
bottom of the table, the Black Employment Equality Indexes
for each job type are listed. Scores below 1.0 on this index
indicate that blacks are poorly represented, while scores above
1.0 indicate that blacks are overrepresented in CBD jobs.

Because of large regional differences between the southern
and non-southern cities, this data is further broken down by
region in Tables 5.2 and 5.3. No other regional differences were
found to be significant among the non-southern cities.

The initial stage of analysis was suggested by findings in the
studies of central city and SMSA labor markets.[1] According to
these studies, blacks have prospered more in manufacturing
centers rather than office centers, but there is evidence that
blacks are getting relatively high proportions of new office and
office-related jobs.

It is clear both in southern and non-southern cities that
blacks are not well represented in the professional, technical,
managerial, or high level clerical types. The Black Employment Equality Indexes never exceed 1.0 in these job categories.
Lack of longitudinal data for CBD employment makes it
impossible to fully assess the progress blacks may have had in
these categories. From the totals in these tables, and from the
data for central cities it is obvious that the progress is extremely
slow in the South. There has been progress in the non-
southern cities, but the blacks are still far from proportional
parity. It might be noted, however, that 14,000 of the 109,000
black women employed in CBDs outside the South are in

**Table 5.1   Distribution of Office and Office-related CBD Workers by Occupation, Race, and Sex: Nation (54 cities), 1970**

|  | Professional Technical Managerial | High-level Clerical | Low-level Clerical | Office-associated Jobs | Service | Total[a] |
|---|---|---|---|---|---|---|
| White Male | 504,000 | 17,500 | 88,200 | 29,700 | 60,700 | 1,162,000 |
| Black Male | 13,200 | 700 | 9,000 | 14,200 | 27,300 | 126,900 |
| White Female | 105,900 | 211,700 | 310,700 | 9,400 | 54,000 | 929,100 |
| Black Female | 6,900 | 16,600 | 52,400 | 5,700 | 25,300 | 153,200 |
| Other Races |  |  |  |  |  |  |
| Male and Female | 10,800 | 3,000 | 9,500 | 900 | 4,900 | 42,700 |
| Male Total | 526,200 | 18,800 | 99,100 | 44,600 | 90,500 | 1,312,400 |
| Female Total | 114,600 | 231,100 | 370,700 | 15,300 | 81,700 | 1,101,500 |
| Black Employment      M | .259 | .384 | .936 | 3.282 | 3.110 |  |
| Equality Index           F | .433 | .518 | 1.017 | 2.680 | 2.228 |  |

[a]The "Total" includes other occupations for which individual figures are not given.

**Table 5.2 Distribution of Office and Office-related CBD Workers by Occupation, Race, and Sex: 32 Non-Southern Cities, 1970**

| | Professional Technical Managerial | High-level Clerical | Low-level Clerical | Office-associated Jobs | Service | Total[a] |
|---|---|---|---|---|---|---|
| White Male | 369,600 | 13,100 | 65,000 | 20,900 | 44,500 | 840,000 |
| Black Male | 10,200 | 900 | 6,700 | 9,200 | 14,500 | 78,400 |
| White Female | 75,700 | 152,300 | 226,200 | 6,700 | 41,700 | 667,600 |
| Black Female | 5,300 | 14,100 | 41,300 | 3,800 | 13,500 | 109,000 |
| Other Races | 10,000 | 2,800 | 9,000 | 900 | 4,800 | 39,800 |
| | | | | | | |
| Total Male | 388,100 | 14,400 | 74,000 | 30,800 | 61,400 | |
| Total Female | 82,700 | 168,800 | 274,200 | 10,700 | 57,600 | |
| | | | | | | |
| Black Employment   M | .313 | .753 | 1.096 | 3.599 | 2.84 | |
| Equality Index   F | .468 | .610 | 1.100 | 2.592 | 1.71 | |

[a] The "Total" includes other occupations for which individual figures are not given.

**Table 5.3   Distribution of Office and Office-related CBD Workers by Occupation, Race, and Sex: 22 Southern Cities, 1970**

| | Professional Technical Managerial | High-level Clerical | Low-level Clerical | Office-associated Jobs | Service | Total[a] |
|---|---|---|---|---|---|---|
| White Male | 134,400 | 4,800 | 23,200 | 8,800 | 16,200 | 322,000 |
| Black Male | 3,000 | 200 | 2,300 | 5,000 | 12,800 | 48,500 |
| White Female | 30,200 | 59,400 | 84,500 | 2,700 | 12,300 | 261,500 |
| Black Female | 1,600 | 2,500 | 11,100 | 1,900 | 11,800 | 44,200 |
| Other Races | 800 | 200 | 500 | 0 | 100 | 2,900 |
| | | | | | | |
| Male Total | 138,100 | 5,200 | 25,600 | 13,800 | 29,100 | |
| Female Total | 31,900 | 61,900 | 96,000 | 4,600 | 24,100 | |
| | | | | | | |
| Black Employment   M | .167 | .296 | .691 | 2.78 | 3.38 | |
| Equality Index   F | .351 | .282 | .808 | 2.88 | 3.42 | |

[a]The "Total" includes other occupations for which individual figures are not given.

these high-level clerical jobs, while another 5,300 are in professional, managerial, or technical jobs.

In the low-level clerical job category, both black women and men are well represented in the non-southern cities. The Black Employment Equality Indexes exceed 1.0 for both sexes. This might be interpreted as a hopeful beginning, especially since many blacks did not have access to the education that would qualify them for these jobs until recently. But it also might be interpreted as an indication that the vast majority of blacks are being restricted to the lowest levels in an occupation which is expanding mostly with low-level jobs. Given the short time in which this movement into white-collar jobs took place, and the signs that black women are filtering into some of the high-level clerical positions, the more optimistic interpretation seems plausible. The second scenario at the end of Chapter 1 showing the labor market absorbing a select group of blacks receives confirmation from this data.

In the South, however, the Black Employment Equality Indexes for low-level clerical jobs remain below 1.0. While the Index for southern women appears to approach parity (it is .808), a detailed breakdown of this category which appears in Appendix B shows that a high percentage are telephone operators. Except in the newer and peripheral cities of the South, black representation is still low.

It is in the office-associated job and service job categories that blacks find their highest representation in office-related jobs. The Black Employment Equality Indexes for both sexes are high both in the southern and non-southern cities. The absolute number of these jobs is not great in comparison to the number of clerical jobs, but many of them are new jobs providing opportunities for blacks in office-dominated sectors of the labor market. Some are dead-end jobs, but for some, like building maintenance, unionization has brought upgrading in status and income.

## Detailed Occupational Patterns in All CBD Jobs

Tables 5.4 and 5.5 present general occupational breakdowns for all CBD workers in non-southern and southern cities respectively. Appendix A breaks the same information further

**Table 5.4   General CBD Occupations by Race and Sex in 32 Non-Southern Cities, 1970**

| | White Male | Percent | Black Male | Percent | White Female | Percent | Black Female | Percent |
|---|---|---|---|---|---|---|---|---|
| Professional and Technical | 234,100 | 27.5 | 7,300 | 9.1 | 65,500 | 9.7 | 7,700 | 7.1 |
| Managers and Administrators | 159,300 | 18.7 | 4,600 | 5.7 | 33,000 | 4.9 | 1,700 | 1.6 |
| Sales Workers | 94,900 | 11.2 | 3,500 | 4.4 | 55,100 | 8.2 | 5,800 | 5.3 |
| High-level Clerical Workers | 13,100 | 1.5 | 900 | 1.1 | 152,300 | 22.6 | 14,100 | 12.9 |
| Low-level Clerical Workers | 65,000 | 7.6 | 6,700 | 8.4 | 226,200 | 33.5 | 41,300 | 37.8 |
| Office-associated, Clerical | 20,900 | 2.6 | 9,200 | 11.5 | 6,700 | 1.0 | 3,800 | 3.5 |
| Clerical, Nonoffice | 27,400 | 3.2 | 2,900 | 3.6 | 42,800 | 6.3 | 7,700 | 7.1 |
| Craftsmen | 105,000 | 12.4 | 9,100 | 11.3 | 9,700 | 1.4 | 1,100 | 1.0 |
| Operatives | 44,900 | 5.3 | 11,400 | 14.2 | 30,900 | 4.6 | 7,800 | 7.1 |
| Laborers | 16,600 | 2.0 | 7,300 | 9.1 | 2,700 | 0.4 | 800 | 0.7 |
| Service Workers | 68,700 | 8.0 | 17,300 | 21.6 | 49,600 | 7.4 | 17,400 | 15.9 |
| Totals | 849,900 | 100.0 | 80,200 | 100.0 | 674,500 | 100.0 | 109,200 | 100.0 |

into 66 occupational categories for non-southern cities by race and sex; Appendix B does the same for the southern cities. This data is estimated with the use of the one percent sample of the whole population available in the Public Use Sample. The smaller numbers that appear in some cells of the appendices are subject to much sampling error. But the aggregate picture is clear enough and reliable enough to recognize patterns by race and sex.[2]

In the professional and managerial categories, most of the blacks are in the categories of nurses, dieticians, therapists, and health technicians in all of the cities, and additionally in the categories of teachers, social and recreation workers, and government administration in the non-southern cities. From the categories just listed, it is not surprising that there are more black women than black men in professional and technical jobs. There is little black representation in the higher paying professional and managerial jobs. In the South, the presence of blacks is negligible in positions such as office manager, sales manager, buyer, physician, dentist, public administrator, lawyer, architect, and civil and industrial engineer.

In all of the cities, blacks are poorly represented in sales positions. Even in the category of retail sales clerk, blacks do not have a proportional share of the jobs. This could be partly the result of the fact that the total number of CBD retailing jobs has dropped off considerably, and that job openings have been few in number. It could also be the result of discrimination by employers keeping blacks out of positions in which they would have close contact with customers.

In clerical jobs, the detailed categories show that although black women are filtering into the high-level clerical positions outside the South, they are still not close to proportional parity with white women in secretarial jobs. While 19.0 percent of the white women employed in the CBD are secretaries, only 7.9 percent of the black women are so employed.

In the category of service workers, the detailed breakdown adds police, health service, and private household workers to the list of service occupations included earlier in Tables 5.1, 5.2, and 5.3. In all the cities, blacks have a large proportion of the jobs in health, cleaning, and private household services. In the south, there are more blacks than whites in cleaning and

Table 5.5  General CBD Occupations by Race and Sex in 22 Southern Cities, 1970

| | White Male | Percent | Black Male | Percent | White Female | Percent | Black Female | Percent |
|---|---|---|---|---|---|---|---|---|
| Professional and Technical | 80,600 | 25.7 | 2,300 | 4.8 | 27,300 | 10.7 | 2,800 | 6.3 |
| Managers and Administrators | 57,800 | 18.5 | 1,500 | 3.1 | 13,100 | 5.1 | 500 | 1.1 |
| Sales Workers | 36,800 | 11.7 | 1,000 | 2.1 | 25,300 | 10.0 | 2,700 | 6.1 |
| High-level Clerical Workers | 4,800 | 1.5 | 200 | 0.4 | 59,400 | 23.2 | 2,500 | 5.7 |
| Low-level Clerical Workers | 23,200 | 7.4 | 2,300 | 4.8 | 81,100 | 31.7 | 11,100 | 25.1 |
| Office-associated, Clerical | 8,800 | 2.8 | 5,000 | 10.5 | 2,700 | 1.1 | 1,900 | 4.3 |
| Clerical, Nonoffice | 9,200 | 2.9 | 1,700 | 3.6 | 18,600 | 7.3 | 2,900 | 6.6 |
| Craftsmen | 43,700 | 14.0 | 3,500 | 7.3 | 2,500 | 1.0 | 500 | 1.1 |
| Operatives | 18,600 | 5.9 | 10,300 | 21.6 | 9,100 | 3.6 | 3,800 | 8.6 |
| Laborers | 6,500 | 2.0 | 6,400 | 13.4 | 800 | 0.3 | 200 | 0.5 |
| Service Workers | 23,200 | 7.4 | 13,500 | 28.3 | 15,900 | 6.2 | 15,300 | 34.6 |
| Totals | 313,200 | 99.8 | 47,700 | 99.9 | 255,800 | 100.2 | 44,200 | 100.0 |

food services. Blacks are underrepresented among the police, although they are getting close to parity in the non-southern cities.

Black males have a very high proportion of the other lower-level blue collar job categories, both in the South and the non-South. Large numbers of blacks are laborers, operatives, and transportation workers. Many of these jobs are low-paying, dead-end jobs. But some offer promise of upgrading through unionization. An occupation showing promise of upgrading is transportation in the South, where there are almost as many blacks as whites employed.

The blacks do not have proportional representation in the high-level blue-collar jobs, notably in the craftsman category. As in retailing jobs, this might be partially explained by the loss in the number of these CBD jobs as companies moved or simply reduced manpower through mechanization. Discrimination might also play a part in excluding blacks from these more lucrative positions. In construction, where downtown building efforts opened up many new jobs in the 1960s, blacks are better represented in the craftsman category. In construction outside the South, the ratio of white craftsmen to blacks is 6 to 1, while the ratio for industrial craftsmen is 14 to 1. A similar pattern is clear in the South.

## Conclusion

These conclusions may be drawn from this information on the CBD workforce:

1) Blacks have obtained few jobs in the professional, technical, managerial, and high level clerical categories except in lower paying health, social service, and governmental positions.

2) In the non-southern cities, black women are obtaining more than their proportional share in a wide range of low-level clerical jobs. There is evidence they are filtering into some of the high-level clerical jobs, although they are still far from proportional parity. In the southern cities, few black women have obtained clerical jobs, except in select categories like telephone operator.

3) In office-related jobs black men and women have obtained more than their proportionate share in all cities. The number of these jobs, at least as they can be differentiated in the census data, is not great. But they are new jobs that have developed to service the growing office sector and which are available for newer migrants or unskilled people.

4) In the sales worker and craftsmen categories, blacks are not well represented in any region. A combination of factors like a tight labor market, discrimination, and lack of skills may combine to cause this. There is evidence that blacks are approaching parity with whites as construction craftsmen, which was a growth category in the CBD of the 1960s.

5) In the low-skilled blue-collar categories like operatives and laborers, blacks are more than proportionately represented.

6) Blacks face a segmented labor market in the CBD, with various levels of wages, advancement possibilities, union protection, and job stability.

## Notes

1. Dale Hiestand, "Minorities," in *New York is Very Much Alive*, ed. Eli Ginzberg (New York: McGraw-Hill, 1973); Louis Loewenstein, *The Location of Residences and Work Places in Urban Areas* (New York: Scarecrow Press, 1965), p. 251.

2. When the estimated number in any of the cells on these tables is 10,000, one can say with 95 percent certainty that the finding in a sample of this size differs by no more than 2,156 cases in either direction from what would have been obtained by counting the whole population. When the estimated number is 500, the confidence interval would be 474 cases in either direction; when the estimated number is 1,000, the confidence interval would be 668 cases in either direction; when the estimated number is 100,000, the confidence interval would be 6, 680 cases in either direction. These confidence intervals were calculated from the approximate standard errors of estimated numbers in the 1 in 100 sample of the Public Use Sample presented in U.S. Bureau of the Census, *Census Data Products, Organization, Access and Use*, vol. 1 (Washington: Department of Commerce, 1970), p. 117.

# 6  The Effects of Age, Sex, and Education

## Sex Differences in CBD Labor Force Participation

Do black women profit more from the availability of job opportunities in the CBD than black men? The data in the previous chapter gives some indications that this is so. This chapter will look at the question in various ways. First of all, the question will be asked whether the level of black employment of either sex is affected by the extent of office expansion in the CBD. For this analysis, a ratio comparing the percentage of all SMSA blacks employed in the CBD to the percentage of all workers employed in the CBD will be used. This ratio will show the black relative share of CBD employment. A ratio higher than 1.00 shows that a higher percentage of blacks have CBD jobs than whites.

Tables 6.1 and 6.2 show the ratios for the non-southern and southern cities, respectively. In the non-southern cities, the female ratio exceeded the male ratio in 17 of the 32 cities, and the ratios were equal in two others. No pattern seems evident until cities with high office concentrations are compared with cities with low office concentrations in the CBD. Table 6.1 ranks the cities by their Office Concentration Indexes (the percentage of office jobs in the CBD labor force). Of the eleven cities where the black male relative share of CBD employment

Table 6.1    Black Relative Share of CBD Employment: 32 Non-Southern Cities, 1970
(Cities Ranked Low to High on CBD Office Concentration Index)

|  | Male | Female |
|---|---|---|
| Flint[a] | .54 | .98 |
| Youngstown | 1.54 | 1.02 |
| Dayton | 1.11 | 1.04 |
| Denver | 1.43 | 1.03 |
| San Diego | .92 | 1.06 |
| Indianapolis | 1.04 | .98 |
| Sacramento | 1.00 | .73 |
| Cincinnati | .77 | .77 |
| Omaha | .68 | .97 |
| Minneapolis | 1.42 | 1.38 |
| Buffalo | .80 | 1.10 |
| Rochester | 1.00 | 1.05 |
| St. Louis | 1.02 | .99 |
| Wichita | .94 | .86 |
| Milwaukee | .78 | .94 |
| Akron | 1.26 | 1.17 |
| Pittsburgh | 1.15 | 1.01 |
| Detroit | 1.00 | 1.47 |
| Cleveland | 1.08 | 1.08 |
| Toledo | .73 | 1.23 |
| Columbus | .85 | 1.10 |
| Philadelphia | .90 | 1.19 |
| San Francisco | .74 | .88 |
| Seattle | 1.02 | 1.17 |
| Newark | 1.23 | 1.46 |
| Chicago | .73 | 1.07 |
| Washington | 1.04 | 1.21 |
| Baltimore | 1.03 | .85 |
| Boston | 1.00 | 1.33 |
| Los Angeles | 1.37 | 1.44 |
| Phoenix | 1.00 | 1.17 |
| Kansas City[b] | .80 | .85 |

[a] Ranks lowest on Office Concentration Index.
[b] Ranks highest on Office Concentration Index.

was higher than the black female share, ten were below the median on the ranking of cities by office concentration. The higher the office concentration in the CBD, the greater the percentage of jobs held by black women. Black men hold more jobs in the CBDs with fewer office jobs.

The black male relative shares of CBD employment for all of

Table 6.2    Black Relative Share of CBD Employment: 22 Southern Cities, 1970
(Cities Ranked Low to High on CBD Office Concentration Index)

| | Male | Female |
|---|---|---|
| Greensboro[a] | 1.26 | .87 |
| New Orleans | .90 | .82 |
| Memphis | .70 | .60 |
| Knoxville | 1.51 | .77 |
| Austin | .94 | .57 |
| San Antonio | .86 | .76 |
| Fort Worth | 1.06 | .63 |
| Tulsa | .87 | .64 |
| Norfolk | 1.15 | .68 |
| Richmond | .95 | .91 |
| Tampa | .93 | .75 |
| Louisville | 1.30 | .92 |
| Birmingham | .82 | .64 |
| Little Rock | .83 | .59 |
| Atlanta | 1.02 | .96 |
| Miami | .62 | .59 |
| Charlotte | .78 | .65 |
| Dallas | .89 | .69 |
| Houston | .82 | .82 |
| Nashville | .91 | .58 |
| Jacksonville | .87 | .56 |
| Oklahoma City[b] | .90 | .62 |

[a] Ranks lowest on Office Concentration Index.
[b] Ranks highest on Office Concentration Index.

the cities in each of the regions puts the picture into perspective. The ratio for women is 1.08 in the non-southern cities and .71 in the southern cities. For men it is 1.00 in the non-southern cities and .95 in the southern cities. The black women in the non-southern states have more than their share of CBD jobs while women in the South have a very small share. In the South, there is little difference between male and female shares among either whites or blacks.

In the southern cities, Table 6.2 shows that black men had a greater relative share than black women in 21 of 22 cities, and in the remaining city (Houston), the ratios were even. Even though a higher percentage of urban white males than black males work in the southern CBDs (indicated by a ratio less than

1.0), black women in the South have an even smaller percentage of CBD jobs. There is no city in the South where the percentage of the black female labor force working in the CBD exceeds the percentage of the white female labor force working there. Black women in the South evidently suffer from the double handicap of race and sex in the CBD labor market. Office concentration does not give black women an advantage in the number or proportion of CBD jobs over black men as it does in the non-southern cities.

The comparison of average salaries by sex, race, and region for CBD and SMSA workers gives another vantage point from which black CBD employment can be evaluated. Table 6.3 gives the data for 54 cities from the 1970 Census.[1] So many locational and occupational categories are combined into these averages that one must be cautious in interpreting them. But the differences between average salaries which appear are consistent with and corroborate the other data in this study.

Black males working in CBDs outside the South earn less on the average than those working elsewhere in the SMSA. The difference between CBD workers and other workers are even greater than they appear in this table, because CBD workers are included in SMSA workers. Not only do black men have a disadvantage in the share of CBD employment, but the quality of jobs they do get is quite low, as much as that can be indicated by income. In the South, black males have equally poor incomes inside and outside the CBD.

Table 6.3    Average Black Salary by Region and Place of Work, 1970

|  |  | Place of Work | |
|  |  | CBD (dollars) | SMSA (dollars) |
| --- | --- | --- | --- |
| Male |  |  |  |
|  | Non-South | $6271 | $6462 |
|  | South | 4838 | 4840 |
| Female |  |  |  |
|  | Non-South | 3884 | 3797 |
|  | South | 2985 | 2839 |

Black women have higher average incomes in the CBD than the rest of the SMSA in both regions. While the earlier data in this chapter showed southern black women at a disadvantage in the number and percentage of CBD jobs they were getting, a more optimistic picture emerges with this earnings data. Although few black women get CBD jobs, some of those who do get them make good salaries in relation to other southern black women. An analysis of data city by city shows that the young black woman is starting to find better CBD employment especially in the rapidly expanding office centers outside the Deep South. Examples are Miami, Dallas, Houston, Jacksonville, and Oklahoma City. The sex differences in CBD employment will continue to emerge as age, education, transportation, and residence factors are sorted out in this chapter and the next.

## The Young Black in the CBD Workforce

The narrowing of the gap between younger black and white workers has been the object of many studies and controversies. Ben Wattenberg and Richard Scammon have been in the forefront of those taking an optimistic view of the narrowing gap, while Michael Flax has raised caution flags about misleading interpretations of such data.[2] The 1970 Census provides age breakdowns on place of work statistics only for the 16–44, the 45–64, and the 65-and-up age brackets.[3] It might be better to examine this question with a 16–35 age group, but it is not possible with available data. Only the Relative Minority Income indicator of occupational standing may be used, since occupational data for place of work is not broken down by age. Relative Minority Income, which is a ratio of black to white income, must be interpreted cautiously, especially for male CBD workers. The average income can be distorted by a disproportionate number of professional and managerial workers. It is valid to use it to compare different age groups.

Table 6.4 shows that younger blacks of both sexes have higher ratios than older blacks in the CBD workforce both in the South and the non-South. The closing of the gap between black and white incomes is especially noticeable among young women in the South. The city by city analysis found this to be

Table 6.4   Ratio of Average Black to Average White Salary
of CBD Workers by Age and by Region, 1970

|  | Male | | Female | |
|---|---|---|---|---|
|  | Non-South | South | Non-South | South |
| CBD Workers |  |  |  |  |
| Age 16–64 | .531 | .445 | .790 | .676 |
| Age 16–44 | .574 | .488 | .803 | .719 |
| Age 45–64 | .496 | .394 | .736 | .570 |

particularly true in the rapidly expanding office centers outside the Deep South, as previously mentioned in the analysis of sex differences.

## The Education of Blacks and CBD Employment

Many are pessimistic about the increased advantage that education can bring to the black person in the labor market. Is finishing high school, community college, or even a four year college program a ticket to a job in our cities? The CBD may be one sector of the labor market where the black person can use his or her education to advantage.

Median years of school completed will be compared for black workers in the CBD, the remainder of the central city, and the fringe for each SMSA. The percentage for CBD workers is expected to be higher than the others. The census provides the median years of education for workers by place of work.[4] Tables 6.5 and 6.6 show these medians.

For black women, the medians for the CBD workers exceed the medians of both the "remainder of central city" workers and the suburban fringe workers in the 45 of 54 cities. In another seven cities, the CBD median is equal to one or both of the other medians. In only two cities, Flint and Wichita, does one of the other medians exceed the CBD median, and that by the slightest of margins.

For males, the CBD median exceeds the other medians in 36 of 54 cities. In another six cities, the CBD median is equal to one of the other medians. In 12 cities, one or both of the other medians exceeds the CBD median. The a's on the table indicate

**Table 6.5** Median Years of School Completed by Blacks in Non-Southern Cities by Place of Work, 1970 (Cities ranked low to high on CBD office concentration index)

| | Males | | | Females | | |
|---|---|---|---|---|---|---|
| | CBD | Remainder | Fringe | CBD | Remainder | Fringe |
| Flint | 11.3 | 11.6[a] | 11.3[b] | 12.2 | 12.3[a] | 12.2[b] |
| Youngstown | 11.0 | 10.9 | 10.6 | 12.2 | 12.1 | 11.8 |
| Dayton | 11.6 | 11.8[a] | 12.2[a] | 12.5 | 12.3 | 12.4 |
| Denver | 12.4 | 12.3 | 12.4[b] | 12.6 | 12.4 | 12.4 |
| San Diego | 12.4 | 12.3 | 12.2 | 12.7 | 12.5 | 12.2 |
| Indianapolis | 12.0 | 11.1 | 11.6 | 12.2 | 12.0 | 11.9 |
| Sacramento | 12.5 | 12.4 | 12.3 | 12.6 | 12.5 | 12.3 |
| Cincinnati | 11.3 | 11.0 | 11.2 | 12.3 | 11.7 | 11.5 |
| Omaha | 12.3 | 11.4 | 12.3[b] | 12.3 | 12.2 | 12.3[b] |
| Minneapolis | 12.6 | 12.3 | 12.1 | 12.5 | 12.2 | 12.5[b] |
| Buffalo | 12.0 | 11.2 | 10.5 | 12.3 | 12.0 | 11.3 |
| Rochester | 10.6 | 11.2[a] | 10.4 | 12.1 | 11.7 | 11.2 |
| St. Louis | 11.4 | 11.1 | 11.1 | 12.3 | 12.0 | 11.6 |
| Wichita | 12.1 | 11.6 | 12.4[a] | 12.2 | 12.2[b] | 12.3[a] |
| Milwaukee | 11.6 | 11.3 | 10.9 | 12.3 | 12.1 | 11.9 |
| Akron | 11.7 | 11.3 | 11.2 | 12.2 | 12.0 | 10.8 |
| Pittsburgh | 12.1 | 11.7 | 11.4 | 12.5 | 12.2 | 12.2 |
| Detroit | 12.3 | 11.4 | 11.3 | 12.5 | 12.2 | 12.1 |
| Cleveland | 12.4 | 11.4 | 11.4 | 12.4 | 12.2 | 11.8 |
| Toledo | 11.8 | 11.1 | 11.7 | 12.3 | 11.9 | 11.4 |
| Columbus | 12.2 | 11.8 | 12.3[a] | 12.4 | 12.2 | 12.1 |
| Philadelphia | 11.7 | 11.2 | 11.3 | 12.2 | 12.1 | 11.7 |
| San Francisco | 12.5 | 12.2 | 12.2 | 12.6 | 12.4 | 12.4 |
| Seattle | 12.5 | 12.2 | 12.4 | 12.3 | 12.3[b] | 12.2 |
| Newark | 12.3 | 11.2 | 11.2 | 12.5 | 12.2 | 11.8 |
| Chicago | 12.4 | 11.8 | 11.4 | 12.5 | 12.3 | 12.0 |
| Washington | 12.3 | 12.1 | 11.7 | 12.5 | 12.3 | 12.1 |
| Baltimore | 10.9 | 10.5 | 11.7 | 12.3 | 11.8 | 11.9 |
| Boston | 12.2 | 12.2[b] | 12.2[b] | 12.4 | 12.3 | 12.2 |
| Los Angeles | 12.6 | 12.3 | 12.3 | 12.7 | 12.5 | 12.5 |
| Phoenix | 12.1 | 11.5 | 12.3[a] | 12.3 | 12.1 | 11.8 |
| Kansas City | 12.1 | 11.6 | 12.0 | 12.2 | 12.2[b] | 12.2[b] |

[a] Median education score exceeds that of CBD.
[b] Median education score equal to that of CBD.

**Table 6.6** Median Years of School Completed by Blacks in Southern Cities by Place of Work, 1970
(Cities ranked low to high on CBD office concentration index)

| | Males | | | Females | | |
|---|---|---|---|---|---|---|
| | CBD | Remainder | Fringe | CBD | Remainder | Fringe |
| Greensboro | 11.5 | 11.0 | 10.1 | 12.2 | 12.1 | 11.4 |
| New Orleans | 11.2 | 9.9 | 9.9 | 12.1 | 11.4 | 10.6 |
| Memphis | 10.2 | 9.9 | 8.8 | 11.8 | 11.2 | 10.3 |
| Knoxville | 10.6 | 11.8[a] | 11.6[b] | 12.3 | 11.7 | 12.0 |
| Austin | 12.1 | 11.4 | 12.1[a] | 12.2 | 12.0 | 11.6 |
| San Antonio | 12.1 | 12.2[a] | 12.1[a] | 12.6 | 12.1 | 11.7 |
| Fort Worth | 11.5 | 10.9[b] | 11.9[b] | 12.1 | 11.4 | 11.5 |
| Tulsa | 12.0 | 12.0[b] | 11.1 | 12.3 | 12.0 | 11.0 |
| Norfolk | 10.2 | 10.6[a] | 9.3 | 12.3 | 11.3 | 10.7 |
| Richmond | 11.0 | 10.2 | 9.7 | 12.0 | 11.1 | 10.7 |
| Tampa | 11.3 | 10.7 | 10.0 | 11.5 | 11.0 | 10.6 |
| Louisville | 11.0 | 10.7 | 11.2[b] | 12.2 | 11.8 | 11.5 |
| Birmingham | 11.7 | 10.6 | 9.9 | 12.5 | 11.9[b] | 11.1 |
| Little Rock | 11.7 | 11.4 | 10.9 | 11.8 | 11.8[b] | 11.0 |
| Atlanta | 12.2 | 11.2 | 11.1 | 12.3 | 12.0 | 10.8 |
| Miami | 11.0 | 10.2 | 10.1 | 12.2 | 11.5 | 10.8 |
| Charlotte | 11.8 | 10.6 | 10.3 | 12.1 | 11.4 | 11.0 |
| Dallas | 11.7 | 11.4 | 10.9 | 12.4 | 12.0 | 10.9 |
| Houston | 11.8 | 11.1 | 10.1 | 12.4 | 12.0[b] | 11.0 |
| Nashville | 11.5 | 11.2[b] | 9.6 | 12.1 | 12.1[b] | 10.8 |
| Jacksonville | 10.8 | 10.8[b] | N.A. | 12.3 | 11.5 | N.A. |
| Oklahoma City | 12.0 | 12.2[a] | 12.1[b] | 12.4 | 12.3 | 12.4[b] |

N.A. = Not Applicable.
[a] Median education score exceeds that of CBD.
[b] Median education score equal to that of CBD.

these latter cities. They are generally the smaller cities in the sample, or the cities with small proportions of blacks. In a dozen of the larger office centers, the CBD median is more than half a year higher than either of the other medians.

It is a hopeful sign that the CBD is providing work for better educated blacks of both sexes in the South and outside the South. Perhaps in time, more young, well-educated blacks will increase the proportional representation of blacks in the CBD workforce.

### Conclusions

1) The amount of office concentration in the CBD had a positive effect on the amount of jobs open to black women in the CBD in cities outside the South. It had a negative effect on the amount of jobs available to men.

2) In the South, the amount of office concentration in the CBD had no apparent effect on the amount of jobs open to black men or women.

3) Black female CBD workers have higher incomes on the average than black women working in other parts of the metropolis. This is true even in the South, indicating that the few blacks who get jobs there are getting relatively good paying jobs.

4) Black male CBD workers have lower incomes on the average than black men working in other parts of the metropolis.

5) The gap between black and white incomes of CBD workers narrows among younger people. It is particularly noticeable among women in souther cities.

6) The CBD offers more employment to better educated blacks of both sexes than any other area of the metropolis.

7) The assimilation of blacks into the various segments of the CBD labor market is very conditional on sex, age, and educational background.

### Notes

1. U.S. Bureau of the Census, *Census of Population, 1970; Detailed Characteristics*, Table 190.

2. Ben J. Wattenberg and Richard M. Scammon, "Black Progress and Liberal Rhetoric," *Commentary* 55 (April 1973); Michael J. Flax, *Blacks and Whites: An Experiment in Racial Indicators* (Washington: The Urban Institute, 1971).

3. U.S. Bureau of the Census, *Census of Population, 1970; Detailed Characteristics,* Table 190.

4. *Ibid.*, Table 190.

# 7 The Effects of Ecological and Labor Market Characteristics

## CBD Office Concentration and the Quality of Black Employment

Previous research on SMSA labor markets indicates that the occupational standing of black CBD workers is inversely related to the proportion of office jobs, although the gap between white and black females is rapidly lessening. Blacks are found to have better occupational standing where industrial and other non-clerical jobs predominate.[1] The CBD data helps us examine one portion of the SMSA labor market. Reference was made in Chapter 1 to many studies adding a locational factor, namely the suburbanization of jobs. The data in this study brings attention to the CBD.

"Occupational standing" is measured in two ways in this analysis. One is the Index of Occupational Dissimilarity (I.D.) and the other is the Relative Minority Income Ratio. Table 7.1 shows the zero order correlations between the CBD Office Concentration Index and these indicators for male CBD workers. Note first that all of the signs are in the predicted direction. A negative sign on the correlation of office concentration with relative minority income indicates a disadvantage for the blacks as office concentration increases. A positive sign on the correlation of office concentration with the Occupational

Table 7.1   Correlations: CBD Office Concentration Index with
Male Black Occupational Standing, 1970

| | Relative Minority Income | | | Occupational ID |
|---|---|---|---|---|
| | Age 16–64 | Age 16–44 | Age 45–64 | |
| All Cities (N=54) | −.231[a] | −.093 | −.325[a] | .054 |
| Non-South (N=32) | −.592[a] | −.260 | −.769[a] | .413[a] |
| South (N=22) | −.312 | −.328 | −.219 | .178 |

[a] Significant at .05.

Index of Dissimilarity also indicates a disadvantaged position for the blacks.

The magnitude of the correlation coefficients for males shows that the inverse relationship between office concentration and the quality of jobs for blacks is substantial and significant only for certain regions or age groups. The coefficients are significant and substantial mainly in non-southern cities and for the older age group. Among older workers in non-southern cities, the coefficient is −.769. This indicates that CBD office concentration is a strong negative predictor of relative minority income for that group of workers.

There are various possible explanations for the differences by region and age. Younger blacks, with better education, may be profiting more from job opportunities in the office sector. The coefficients for southern cities may be lower because there is discrimination against blacks across most sectors of the labor market, while the non-southern cities may have differential rates of opportunity for blacks in the various labor market sectors. In other words, southern blacks have equally low occupational standing, no matter what type of economic activity is dominant. This is shown by the fact that the variances on all the income and occupational indicators are lower in the southern than in the non-southern cities.

Another consideration must be present when interpreting

Table 7.2    Correlation Matrix of SMSA Characteristics and CBD
Office Concentration Index, 1970

|  |  | 2 | 3 | 4 | 5 | 6 |
|---|---|---|---|---|---|---|
| 1. Population Size | N–S | .420[a] | .604[a] | .010 | .160 | .428[a] |
|  | S | .094 | .261 | .039 | .019 | .186 |
| 2. Percent Black | N–S |  | .484[a] | .271 | .102 | .205 |
|  | S |  | .548[a] | .483[a] | -.252 | -.197 |
| 3. Percent Public Transp. | N–S |  |  | .126 | .016 | .442[a] |
|  | S |  |  | .231 | -.540[a] | -.384[a] |
| 4. Black Centrality | N–S |  |  |  | .052 | .150 |
|  | S |  |  |  | -.059 | .168 |
| 5. Residential Segregation | N–S |  |  |  |  | .160 |
|  | S |  |  |  |  | .477[a] |
| 6. CBD Office | N–S |  |  |  |  |  |
| Concentration | S |  |  |  |  |  |

N–S = Non-South; S = South.

[a] Significant at .05.

these correlations. The pattern of correlations of the CBD
Office Concentration Index with other ecological and racial
characteristics of the city differs in southern and non-southern
cities. Table 7.2 reveals that in non-southern cities, CBD office
concentration is related to city population size (r=.428) and to
the percent of public transportation users (r=.442). In the
south, office concentration is not related to city size, and it has a
negative relation to the percent of public transportation users
(r=-.384). While these coefficients are not large, they do show
that the Index of Office Concentration indicates more than just
occupational type. In later analysis, key ecological and racial
characteristics will be controlled in regression analysis.

Among female CBD workers, small and insignificant correlations were obtained with relative minority income. A
pattern of insignificant correlations was found in the relation
of this variable to other variables. With region controlled,
relative minority income had less variance than the corresponding indicator for males. Since the average salary of black
women is low and relatively constant in relation to the average

salary of white women, it is a poor indicator to use in regression analysis.

The Index of Occupational Dissimilarity, however, does show many significant correlations for women. Its correlation with office concentration is -.383 for all cities in the sample. The negative sign indicates that the greater the percentage of office workers in the CBD, the less the dissimilarity between occupational distributions of black and white women. Whereas CBD office concentration has a disadvantageous effect on black men, it has an advantageous effect on black women. In the 22 southern cities, the correlation was -.493, while the 32 non-southern cities, it was -.239 (which was significant only at the .09 level). The fact that the correlation in the south was higher than that for the nation may be explained in part by the fact that rapidly growing cities outside the Deep South had the highest rank on the Office Concentration Index. Examples of these are Miami, Dallas, Houston, Jacksonville, and Oklahoma City.

Further data from this study shows that in the non-southern cities, the percent of clerical jobs in the SMSA is a strong negative predictor of male relative minority income (r=.617), while in the South it is not so strong (-.125). Again, for women, insignificant correlations were found with relative minority income. The Index of Occupational Dissimilarity was not calculated for the SMSA workforce. At least for men, for whom we have good indicators, the same pattern of relations between the percent of office jobs and occupational standing is found in CBD and SMSA workforces.

## Public Transportation and Black CBD Employment

Is black participation in the CBD workforce dependent on the availability of public transportation to the core? Meyer, Kain, and Wohl, after intensive study of the relation between workplace and residence, conclude that "within income and housing constraints, negroes display about the same housing and transportation choices as whites."[2] But income and housing constraints, they say, differ between the races. Segregation forces the black to pay more for housing, and the segegated housing is closer to the CBD. This leaves less for transportation costs, and brings more reliance on public transportation.[3]

The question has a practical policy implication. Public subsidy of mass transit has often been justified because of supposed benefits to the poor. Martin Wohl, however, claims that many mass transit improvements have aided only a very small percentage of suburban middle and upper class workers.[4] This could be the outcome of an upgrading of long distance commuter services rather than transportation services for the inner city. But it could also be a result of a lack of demand or need by inner-city residents.

The possible dependency of inner-city blacks on public transportation will be analyzed in two ways. First, the black relative share of CBD employment (the ratio of the percentage of SMSA black workers employed in the CBD to the percentage of all SMSA workers employed in the CBD) will be correlated with the percentage of CBD workers using public transportation. The 1970 Census provided information on the percentage of CBD workers using public transportation in each of the 54 sample cities.[5] The same census tables provided average incomes for public transportation users among CBD workers. This will provide data for the second kind of analysis which will look at the income levels of CBD workers that use public transportation.

The correlations between black relative share of CBD employment and the percent of public transportation users to the CBD do not provide any evidence that public transportation availability affects black males. Table 7.3 shows that none of the coefficients for men are significant. For black women, the correlation is small but significant (r=.296) in non-southern cities. The coefficient (.296) is similar in southern cities but significant only at the .09 level. The availability of public transportation to the CBD does slightly increase the black women's share of CBD jobs.

The correlation for black women in all cities (r=.522) is spuriously high. The reason is that southern cities have low relative CBD shares and low public transportation use. When these cities are included with non-southern cities which have higher scores on both variables, a spurious correlation appears which disappears when a control for region is introduced.

In the second stage of analysis, the average salary of black public transportation users to the CBD is compared to the average salary of all black CBD workers. Table 7.4 shows the

Table 7.3   Correlation of Percent Public Transportation Use
and Relative Black Share of CBD Jobs, 1970

|  | Male | Female |
|---|---|---|
| All Cities | -.080 | .522[a] |
| (N=54) | (s=.283) | (s=.001) |
| Non-South | -.116 | .296[a] |
| (N=32) | (s=.265) | (s=.050) |
| South | -.246 | .296 |
| (N=22) | (s=.135) | (s=.090) |

[a]Significant at .05.

average salaries by age, sex, and transportation use for 29 cities for which data were available in all categories.

In all categories, the average salary of public transportation users was below that of all CBD workers. The differences are substantial, especially when one considers that the category of "all CBD workers" includes the public transportation users. It is the low paid worker who depends on public transportation. The higher income earners are more likely to use private transportation. Whether the volume of this usage demands more public services or subsidies depends on a careful cost-benefit analysis. Usually some public transportation service is

Table 7.4   Average Salary for Black CBD Workers, by Transportation
Use, Region, Age, and Sex, 1970

|  | Age 16–44 | | Age 45–64 | |
|---|---|---|---|---|
|  | Use Public Transportation (dollars) | All CBD Workers (dollars) | Use Public Transportation (dollars) | All CBD Workers (dollars) |
| Non-South (16 Cities) | | | | |
| Male | 4366 | 6058 | 5816 | 6858 |
| Female | 3524 | 3971 | 4000 | 4644 |
| South (13 Cities) | | | | |
| Male | 3242 | 4799 | 4079 | 5166 |
| Female | 2476 | 3103 | 2591 | 3279 |

in place to serve inner city residential areas. The cost-benefit analysis should determine whether its continuance or improvement is justified. A discontinuance of service would definitely hurt the low income black worker.

## The Relationship Between Residential Segregation and Workplace

In studies to date, the relationship between residential segregation and black occupational standing has not been clear. Does a relationship exist? If so, in which direction do lines of causality flow? Jerolyn Lyle could not find any significant statistical relationship between the two for men, and only a low inverse relationship for women.[6] In an intensive study of the relationship in Detroit and Chicago, John Kain finds "highly tentative" evidence that housing market segregation adversely affects the level of black employment.[7] He theorizes that housing segregation puts constraints on job opportunities, by reducing access to and communications about job placements.

Stanley Friedlander, on the other hand, found some evidence that high segregation was associated with low unemployment for blacks.[8] He speculates that this could be the result of a more effective labor market information system because of the forced cohesiveness and closeness of people in the black ghetto. It could also be from a reduced level of competition for central city jobs as whites have moved away from the central city.

These results are not necessarily contradictory. Some deal with the quantity of black jobs, some with quality, and some with unemployment rates. This study does not hope to answer the larger question, but it can isolate one segment of the labor market (the CBD). Correlation-regression analysis will be used to study the relationship between segregation and black occupational standing.

The Sorensen, Taueber, and Hollingsworth Indexes of Block Residential Segregation for Whites and Negroes in 1970 are used as indicators of segregation. These were reported in Tables 3.3 and 3.4. An index score is available for all of the 54 cities in this study except for Phoenix. These index scores will be correlated with the Relative Minority Income Ratio and the

Index of Occupational Dissimilarity for CBD workers by sex and region. The SMSA Relative Minority Income Ratios will also be correlated with segregation.

When region is controlled, Table 7.5 demonstrates that most of the correlations with indicators of black occupational standing are insignificant. The table shows that the correlations for "all cities" disappear when region is controlled except with CBD relative minority income in the South. The correlation for all cities is spuriously high. The southern cities generally have high indexes of residential segregation and poor black occupational standing. The non-southern cities have relatively low indexes of segregation and higher black occupational standing. Mixing all cities brings about the spurious correlation.

When interpreting these results, one factor should be kept in mind. There is little variance in the Taeuber block index of residential segregation for blacks and whites. In the 22 southern cities in the sample for this study, all but New Orleans fell within the range of 89.7, and 95.9. New Orleans was 83.9. With so little variance, correlation-regression analysis will not produce high coefficients. There may be a relationship there

Table 7.5   Correlations of Occupational Indicators with Residential Segregation, 1970

|  | All Cities | Non-South | South |
|---|---|---|---|
| **Male** | | | |
| CBD Relative Minority Income | -.493[a] | -.226 | -.135 |
| SMSA Relative Minority Income | -.442[a] | -.050 | .189 |
| CBD Index of Occupational Dissimilarity | .467[a] | .053 | .048 |
| **Female** | | | |
| CBD Relative Minority Income | -.416[a] | .176 | -.454[a] |
| SMSA Relative Minority Income | -.466[a] | .169 | .066 |
| CBD Index of Occupational Dissimilarity | .503[a] | .268 | -.317 |

[a] Significant at .05.

Negative correlations with Relative Minority Income indicate that higher levels of segregation are associated with poorer relative income of blacks.

Positive correlations with the Index of Occupational Dissimilarity indicate that higher levels of segregation are associated with less black participation in the better occupational categories.

which regression analysis cannot discover with the present data. When longitudinal data becomes available after the 1980 census on CBD workers, that data may show relationships that cannot be seen with cross-sectional data.

The only variables that had significant correlations with the segregation index were some of the occupational characteristics of the city. In non-southern cities, the segregation index correlated at -.314 with percent government jobs in the city, at .335 with percent wholesaling jobs in the city, and at .314 with percent manufacturing jobs in the CBD. The magnitude of these correlations does not allow us to conclude much more than there is some poorly definable link between segregation and occupational characteristics of the city.

## Black Residential Centrality and CBD Employment

If blacks have a larger relative share of CBD jobs, do they tend to live closer to the CBD? The concentration of black residential areas near the CBD is obvious in many cities, but it is not clear whether this is related to location of jobs. Meyer, Kain, and Wohl found in Chicago and Detroit that centrally employed nonwhites lived closer to the center than centrally employed whites. This was found to be true when comparing blacks and whites living in each of three housing types: one-family homes, two-family homes, and multiple family homes.[9] By comparing within the housing types, Meyer, Kain, and Wohl have a rough control for class. This enables them to argue that it is housing discrimination that keeps blacks living closer to the CBD than whites of equal status.

But it still remains to be seen whether there is a link between residential centralization and workplace. The only direct relationship between workplace and population have been found by Black and Lipton, who found pockets of middle class resettlement or renovation of inner city housing close to CBDs dominated by white-collar employment.[10]

The regression analysis was done with the Index of Centrality, prepared for 49 cities out of the 54 cities in this study's sample that had one CBD. The values of this index appear in Tables 3.3 and 3.4.

The correlation between black centralization and relative share of the CBD workforce is .403 for women in non-southern cities. The correlation is insignificant for men in all cities, and for women in the southern cities. It is impossible to say which variable causes the other for the non-southern women. We cannot say whether place of work follows place of residence or vice versa, but we do know they are related. Usually in residential mobility studies, male job location is a better predictor of residential locations than female employment. It is not so in this case.

Black residential centrality is related, like the segregation index, to occupational characteristics of the city. It correlates at .369 with percent in manufacturing jobs in non-southern cities. It is also linked to percent black in the SMSA. In the south, black centrality correlates at .483 with percent black; in non-southern cities, they correlate at .271 (significant at .07). This is similar to the finding by Redick in the original centrality study. The higher the percentage of blacks in an SMSA, the more they tend to be centralized residentially.

Centrality is negatively related to percent Spanish (r=-.368 in the non-South and -.399 in the South). Evidently, the Spanish population competes for housing in the inner city, and this has the effect of dispersing the black population.

## Conclusions

1) There is an inverse relation between the quality of black male employment and office concentration in the CBD. The disadvantage, however, is very much lessened among young blacks outside the South.

2) The quality of black female jobs improves with increased office concentration in the CBD. This was true even in the rapidly growing cities of Florida and Texas in the South. Young black women are getting closer to income parity with young white women.

3) There is a small but significant correlation between the availability of public transportation and the share of CBD employment held by black women. There is no correlation for black males. Among black commuters to the CBD, it is the lower income workers who are more likely to use public transportation.

4) No relation was found between levels of residential segregation and relative measures of black occupational standing.

5) Outside the South, when black women have a higher relative share of CBD jobs, they tend to live closer to the CBD. This was indicated by a moderate correlation between the residential centrality of the black population and the relative share of the CBD jobs. Blacks are more centralized in metropolitan areas with high percentages of blacks. Blacks are less centralized when the percentage of Hispanics is high. The residential centrality of black CBD workers offers a glimmer of hope that these people will remain and help to stabilize and rehabilitate inner-city neighborhoods.

## Notes

1. Jerolyn Ross Lyle, "Differences in the Occupational Standing of Negroes Among Industries and Cities," (Ph.D. Dissertation, University of Maryland, 1970), pp. 64-65 and 82-83.

2. J. R. Meyer, J. F. Kain and M. Wohl, *The Urban Transportation Problem* (Cambridge: Harvard University Press, 1965), p. 162.

3. *Ibid.*, pp. 155-163.

4. Martin Wohl, "Users of Urban Transportation Services and Their Income Circumstances," *Traffic Quarterly* 24 (January 1970), pp. 21-44.

5. U.S. Bureau of the Census, *Census of Population, 1970; Detailed Characteristics*, Table 190.

6. Lyle, *op. cit.*, p. 81.

7. John T. Kain, "Housing Segregation, Negro Employment, and Metropolitan Decentralization," *Quarterly Journal of Economics* 82 (May 1968), p. 190.

8. Stanley Friedlander, *Unemployment in the Urban Core* (New York: Praeger, 1972).

9. Meyer, Kain, and Wohl, *op. cit.* pp. 155-159.

10. Thomas J. Black, "Private-Market Housing Renovation in Central Cities" *Urban Land* 34 (November 1975), pp. 3-9; S. Gregory Lipton, "Evidence of Central City Revival," *Journal of the American Institute of Planners* 43 (April 1977), pp. 136-147.

# 8 Multivariate Analysis

## Explaining the Variation in CBD Black-White Occupational Differences

Various studies have explained much of the variance in urban black-white occupational differences by characteristics of the labor market. Stanley Friedlander found black unemployment in the inner city inversely related to the amount of service and government sector jobs.[1] Jerolyn Lyle found that industrial characteristics of cities explained more of the variance in black-white employment differentials than personal characteristics such as education.[2]

Will the same findings appear in the CBD workforce? Stepwise regression is the procedure to be used in the analysis of this question. Relative Minority Income and the Occupational Index of Dissimilarity will be used, in turn, as dependent variables. Stepwise regression has two advantages at this point. It shows the influence of each independent variable with the others controlled, and it also reveals the relative impact of the independent variables. The stepwise regressions were run with six different combinations of independent variables before the best combination was found. This was not an effort to maximize the cumulative R square. That remained relatively constant for each of the dependent variables through the six series of regressions. Rather, it was an effort to reduce multicollinearity and allow for a better interpretation of the relative influence of key variables examined in the earlier analysis.

Factor analysis was also used in the process of eliminating multicollinearity and picking the best and most clearly interpretable indicators. Appendix C discusses the factor analysis in detail. Appendix C also discusses the procedure by which the linearity assumption for regression analysis was checked, and the reasons why other multivariate statistical models were not suitable for this data.

The independent variables chosen were the CBD office concentration index, the CBD percentage in government jobs, relative black education, percentage black in the SMSA, and percentage using public transportation to the CBD. Unless otherwise indicated, all the data were taken from the 1970 census.[3]

The percentage of workers in construction was not used because it loaded on many factors, indicating a high correlation with other variables in the study. Such correlation among independent variables could produce misleading results in regression analysis. The percentage in retailing was eliminated for the same reason. The percentage in manufacturing did not load on other factors. But it had to be eliminated because the areas designated by the Bureau of the Census as CBD areas may or may not have included the manufacturing area on the fringe of the CBD. By definition, the census CBD does not have to include manufacturing areas. In trial regression runs, there were inconsistencies when this variable was included.

Three clear and independent demographic and ecological indicators were used. Relative black education was measured by the ratio of the number of blacks finishing high school to the number of whites finishing high school. This indicator has been used in similar studies, especially by Lyle.

Three sets of regressions will be reported for each dependent variable. The first will be for all the 54 cities in the sample. This will have a dummy variable for region, (South=0; non-South=1). This dummy variable is essential because of the large differences in the occupational standing indicators or dependent variables by region. The same regression, minus the dummy variable, will be repeated for non-southern and southern cities.

Both unstandardized and standardized (betas) regression coefficients are reported along with the cumulative R square. A direct comparison of betas between the regressions for different regions should not be done because of limitations in the data discussed in Appendix C. For example, it would not be correct to say that the availability of public transportation had a greater effect in the non-southern cities simply because the beta for the non-southern cities was greater than that for the southern cities. But by looking at the beta and the increase in cumulative R square, it is possible to see a rough ordering of the effects contributed by the independent variables.

Tables 8.1 and 8.2 indicate the regressions for Relative

Table 8.1    Stepwise Regression Results: Male CBD Workers: Dependent Variable—Relative Minority Income

| | b | beta | Cumulative R Square |
|---|---|---|---|
| **All Cities** | | | |
| Region (South=0; Non-South=1) | 9.385[a] | .678 | .385 |
| CBD Office Concentration | -.570[a] | -.333 | .532 |
| Percent Public Transportation | -.076 | -.154 | .579 |
| CBD Percent Government Jobs | .192[a] | .178 | .601 |
| Relative Black Education | .070 | .098 | .615 |
| Percent Black in SMSA | -.061 | -.069 | .617 |
| **Non-South** | | | |
| CBD Office Concentration | -.616[a] | -.490 | .351 |
| Percent Public Transportation | -.058 | -.176 | .415 |
| CBD Percent Government Jobs | .122 | .165 | .426 |
| Percent Black in SMSA | -.144 | -.158 | .441 |
| Relative Black Education | -.017 | -.027 | .442 |
| **South** | | | |
| CBD Percent Government Jobs | .523[a] | .473 | .183 |
| Relative Black Education | .221[a] | .407 | .365 |
| CBD Office Concentration | -.556[a] | -.344 | .458 |
| Percent Public Transportation | -.226 | -.234 | .485 |
| Percent Black in SMSA | .092 | .139 | .495 |

[a] Significant at .05.

Table 8.2    Stepwise Regression Results: Male CBD Workers: Dependent
Variable—Occupational Index of Dissimilarity

|  | b | beta | Cumulative R Square |
|---|---|---|---|
| **All Cities** | | | |
| Region (South=0; Non-South=1) | 10.681[a] | -.758 | .536 |
| CBD Office Concentration | .388[a] | .223 | .588 |
| Percent Black in SMSA | .131 | .147 | .603 |
| Relative Black Education | .048 | .065 | .606 |
| Percent Public Transportation | .027 | .055 | .607 |
| CBD Percent Government Jobs | .031 | .028 | .608 |
| **Non-South** | | | |
| CBD Office Concentration | .448[a] | .387 | .171 |
| CBD Percent Government Jobs | .128 | .188 | .200 |
| Percent Public Transportation | .031 | .102 | .207 |
| Relative Black Education | .039 | .066 | .211 |
| **South** | | | |
| Percent Public Transportation | .212 | .264 | .086 |
| CBD Office Concentration | .416 | .310 | .160 |
| Percent Black in SMSA | .163 | .299 | .184 |
| CBD Percent Government Jobs | -.168 | -.182 | .222 |
| Relative Black Education | .052 | .115 | .229 |

[a] Significant at .05.

Minority Income and the Occupational Index of Dissimilarity.
Region explains the greatest part of the variance in the
regression for all cities. After that office concentration has the
largest standardized regression coefficients in most instances.
Note that its effect on black occupational standing is inverse
(indicated by negative signs on Table 8.1 and positive signs on
Table 8.2). Percent government jobs also have moderately
large betas, especially on Relative Minority Income. In the
South, it is a strong positive indicator (beta=.473).

The effect of the government job sector may appear surprising since in most cities it is not a very large percentage of
the work force. Bennett Harrison notes that it has been a
significant source of jobs to minorities.[4] It was also a source of
many new jobs during the government employment expansion of the 1960s. Generally, public employment insures better
tenure for minorities than private employment, and it is also

more secure against sharp cyclical variations. Louis Lowenstein adds a reason why we might expect that CBD government employment would have a significant effect on black employment.[5] He finds public administration jobs more centralized in the city than any of the other major industrial categories. Most government jobs, then, are near the residences of inner-city minorities.

Education has a relatively minor effect except in the South. This is a positive predictor. But its effect is minor compared to the occupational indicators. Availability of transportation and percent black in the SMSA had no significant regression coefficients for the men.

Table 8.3 displays the regressions for Relative Minority Income among women. As noted previously, little variance can be explained in this variable. The analysis will be made from Table 8.4 where the Index of Occupational Dissimilarity is the

Table 8.3   Stepwise Regression Results: Female CBD Workers: Dependent Variable—Relative Minority Income

|  | b | beta | Cumulative R Square |
|---|---|---|---|
| **All Cities** |  |  |  |
| Region (South=0, Non-South=1) | 13.060[a] | .671 | .556 |
| Relative Black Education | .201[a] | .175 | .590 |
| CBD Office Concentration | -.244 | -.101 | .597 |
| CBD Percent Government Jobs | -.086 | -.057 | .602 |
| Percent Public Transportation | .031 | .065 | .604 |
| Percent Black in SMSA | -.028 | -.023 | .605 |
| **Non-South** |  |  |  |
| Relative Black Education | .394[a] | .357 | .129 |
| CBD Percent Government Jobs | -.126 | -.126 | .150 |
| Percent Black in SMSA | -.101 | -.082 | .158 |
| CBD Office Concentration | -.075 | -.044 | .160 |
| **South** |  |  |  |
| Relative Black Education | .112 | .210 | .043 |
| CBD Office Concentration | -.263 | -.176 | .083 |
| Percent Public Transportation | .068 | .159 | .105 |
| CBD Percent Government Jobs | -.050 | -.048 | .107 |
| Percent Black in SMSA | -.030 | -.049 | .109 |

[a]Significant at .05.

Table 8.4    Stepwise Regression Results: Female CBD Workers: Dependent
Variable—Index of Occupational Dissimilarity

|  | b | beta | Cumulative R Square |
|---|---|---|---|
| **All Cities** | | | |
| Region (South=0; Non-South=1) | -12.521[a] | -.516 | .551 |
| Percent Public Transportation | -.129[a] | -.217 | .600 |
| Relative Black Education | -.328[a] | -.229 | .631 |
| CBD Office Concentration | -.591[a] | -.197 | .666 |
| CBD Percent Government Jobs | -.266[a] | -.142 | .686 |
| Percent Black in SMSA | -.032 | -.021 | .687 |
| **Non-South** | | | |
| Percent Public Transportation | -.158[a] | -.411 | .235 |
| Relative Black Education | -.449[a] | -.363 | .350 |
| CBD Percent Government Jobs | -.260 | -.232 | .416 |
| CBD Office Concentration | -.258 | -.136 | .429 |
| Percent Black in SMSA | -.062 | -.045 | .430 |
| **South** | | | |
| CBD Office Concentration | -1.252[a] | -.526 | .243 |
| Relative Black Education | -.177 | -.209 | .260 |
| CBD Percent Government Jobs | -.238 | -.146 | .271 |
| Percent Public Transportation | -.097 | -.144 | .288 |

[a]Significant at .05.

dependent variable. Among women, the effect of education is greater than it was among men. The betas are -.229 in all cities, -.363 in the non-South, and -.209 in the South (again a negative sign indicates an advantageous position for the black). The occupational indicators generally show moderate coefficients. In the South, however, the Office Concentration Index has a high beta (-.526). This apparently is due to growing office centers outside the Deep South offering better opportunities to blacks. In the non-southern cities, transportation contributes more explained variance than any of the other variables.

Among black male CBD workers, the occupational indicators are the key ones, with a high percentage of government jobs having a negative effect. Education generally had insigwork having a negative effect. Education generally had insignificant or small effects compared to those for black women.

Availability of transportation also has beneficial effects for women outside the South, whereas it showed no significant relationships with black male indicators.

### Explaining the Variation in SMSA Black-White Occupational Differences

This analysis is being done to see if the CBD workforce differed in any major way from the SMSA workforce. Do the variables relate to each other in the same way in both workforces? In the SMSA analysis, the percentage of women in clerical jobs is substituted for an office concentration index. The use of percent in manufacturing as an independent variable is possible in the SMSA analysis, whereas it presented measurement reliability problems in the CBD. The dependent variable used is the Relative Minority Income Ratio for SMSA workers. SMSA data is taken from the same 54 cities from which CBD data was taken.

Excluding the new independent variable, the other variables related to each other in almost identical ways in the SMSA and CBD workforces (cf. Tables 8.5 and 8.6). As expected, percent manufacturing in the SMSA workforce had a strong positive relationship with black male occupational standing, and a moderate positive relationship with female occupational standing.

The percentage of the CBD or SMSA workforce that was black was never found to have a significant relation with occupational standing in the regressions. There have been various predictions of greater market discrimination when the black population is large relative to the white. The evidence in this study is similar to the evidence found by Stanley Masters. The data do not support the predictions.

### Conclusions

1) The stepwise regression corroborates the earlier analysis in showing that black men have a poorer position in income and occupational status relative to white men in the CBD as the percentage of CBD office workers increases. Regression analysis did not reveal any relations between black occupational

Table 8.5   Stepwise Regression Results: Male SMSA Workers: Dependent
Variable—Relative Minority Income

|  | b | beta | Cumulative R Square |
|---|---|---|---|
| **All Cities** | | | |
| Region (South=0; Non-South=1) | 7.198[a] | .503 | .542 |
| SMSA Percent Manufacturing | .348[a] | .455 | .626 |
| Percent Black in SMSA | -.195[a] | -.216 | .666 |
| SMSA Percent Government | .536[a] | .319 | .715 |
| SMSA Percent Female Clerical | -.311 | -.157 | .733 |
| Percent Public Transportation | -.075 | -.059 | .735 |
| Relative Black Education | .024 | .031 | .736 |
| **Non-South** | | | |
| SMSA Percent Manufacturing | .428[a] | .879 | .389 |
| Percent Public Transportation | -.122 | -.162 | .545 |
| Relative Black Education | .105 | .193 | .591 |
| Percent Black in SMSA | -.242[a] | -.316 | .607 |
| SMSA Percent Government Jobs | .356[a] | .361 | .647 |
| SMSA Percent Female Clerical | -.132 | -.099 | .650 |
| **South** | | | |
| SMSA Percent Government Jobs | 1.244[a] | .881 | .169 |
| SMSA Percent Manufacturing | .504[a] | .706 | .443 |
| SMSA Percent Clerical | -.196 | -.135 | .458 |
| Percent Black in SMSA | -.115 | -.183 | .471 |
| Relative Black Education | -.077 | -.148 | .477 |
| Percent Public Transportation | -.030 | -.025 | .477 |

[a] Significant at .05.

standing and public transportation availability. A minor positive relationship between level of education and black male occupational standing appeared in the regression analysis.

2) The stepwise regression results also corroborates the analysis in earlier chapters in showing that the occupational status of black women improves as the percentage of office workers in the CBD increases. With black women, there are discernible positive effects of public transportation availability and relative educational achievement.

## Notes

1. Stanley L. Friedlander, *Unemployment in the Urban Core* (New York: Praeger, 1972), p. 94.

Table 8.6    Stepwise Regression Results: Female SMSA Workers:
Dependent Variable—Relative Minority Income

| | b | beta | Cumulative R Square |
|---|---|---|---|
| All Cities | | | |
| Region (South=0; Non-South=1) | 12.828[a] | .611 | .711 |
| Relative Black Education | .339[a] | .273 | .789 |
| Percent Public Transportation | .331[a] | .178 | .802 |
| SMSA Percent Manufacturing | .159 | .142 | .805 |
| SMSA Percent Government Jobs | .279 | .113 | .809 |
| Percent Black in SMSA | -.132 | -.099 | .813 |
| SMSA Percent Female Clerical | -.118 | -.040 | .814 |
| Non-South | | | |
| Relative Black Education | .458[a] | .494 | .256 |
| Percent Public Transportation | .201 | .197 | .305 |
| SMSA Percent Manufacturing | .244 | .372 | .351 |
| SMSA Percent Female Clerical | .383 | .213 | .360 |
| Percent Black in SMSA | -.101 | -.098 | .367 |
| South | | | |
| Relative Black Education | .166 | .324 | .344 |
| SMSA Percent Government Jobs | .785[a] | .599 | .446 |
| SMSA Percent Manufacturing | .333 | .504 | .522 |
| SMSA Percent Female Clerical | -.256 | -.189 | .538 |
| Percent Public Transportation | .288 | .265 | .557 |
| Percent Black In SMSA | -.167 | -.285 | .594 |

[a]Significant at .05.

2. Jerolyn Lyle, "Differences in the Occupational Standing of Negroes Among Industries and Cities",(Ph.D. dissertation, University of Maryland, 1970), pp. 40-49.

3. The source of data for the black percentage of SMSA population was U.S. Bureau of the Census, *Census of Population and Housing, 1970; Census Tracts*, Table P-1; remaining data from *Census of Population, 1970; Detailed Characteristics*, Tables 190 and 197.

4. Bennett Harrison, *Public Employment and Urban Poverty* (Washington, D.C.: The Urban Institute, 1971), p. 27.

5. Louis Loewenstein, *The Location of Residences and Work Places in Urban Areas* (New York: Scarecrow Press, 1965), pp. 83-85.

6. Stanley Masters, *Black-White Income Differentials* (New York: Academic Press, 1975), pp. 84-85.

# 9    Summary

## The Impact on Black Employment

Any conclusions from this study have to be examined against the larger context of structural employment patterns. The percentage of office jobs in the national labor force has been increasing since the 1950s. While the increase is not so rapid now as in the 1950s, it is not clear when the percentage will crest. Accompanying this, there has been a marked slowdown since the 1950s in the growth of semi-skilled and low-skilled jobs typically held by men.

Both of these trends have affected the shape of the city, particularly the CBD. The start of these trends occurred when the black migration from the rural south to the inner cities was at its peak. In view of these structural changes in the labor market, we cannot assume that the absorption of blacks into the urban economy will parallel that of the earlier migrant groups to the city. We are far enough into the history that the patterns, and relationships between the black experience and the labor market change, can be deciphered.

The differential impact of CBD change on black men and women is an unavoidable conclusion. Outside the South black women get a larger share of CBD employment both in relation to white women and black men as the percentage of office jobs in the CBD increases. The gap between the relative income and status of black and white women is also lessened as the percentage of office jobs in the CBD increases. Black women are getting more than their proportionate share of low-level CBD clerical jobs, and are starting to filter into some of the high-level clerical jobs. When the incomes of black women are averaged in each of the metropolitan work localities, the CBD workers have the highest average. In the southern cities, black women are being absorbed into the CBD workforce more slowly, although Florida and Texas in particular show signs of black progress similar to the non-southern cities.

The trends are quite different for black men. This study could not find evidence that their relative share of CBD employment was either increased or decreased by office concentration. But in both measures of relative occupational standing with whites, the gap between black and white increased as office concentration increased. Black men have been obtaining access to some of the service and office related jobs that have opened up in the CBD. Since these were new jobs, as opposed to the older blue-collar jobs in the CBD, a new migrant group had more access to them. The number of these jobs does not appear to be that great, and they are often low paying jobs. Some of these job categories, like building maintenance, have experienced some upgrading in salary.

While important indicators show that the black male is at a disadvantage in the CBD workforce, there are two hopeful signs which may bring a long-term reversal of this trend. One is that the gap between black and white incomes is lessened among younger CBD workers, and similarly, the Index of Occupational Dissimilarity is less among young workers in the CBD. The other is that better educated black men are finding more employment in the CBD than in other parts of the city.

It is important to pay attention to these signs even though their impact may not be too apparent in overall black employment statistics. Peter Blau and Otis Dudley Duncan found that the first full-time job held by a person is the best predictor of his future employment patterns. So attention must be paid to the first jobs being held by younger, better educated blacks.[1]

In the relationship between workplace and residence, when black women had a greater relative share of CBD jobs, the black population resided closer to the center of the city. There was no association between the relative share of CBD jobs by black men and the residential centralization of the black population. There was a small but significant correlation between public transportation use and the black female relative share of CBD jobs.

When the racial compositions of the workforces in the CBD, the remainder of the central city, and the suburbs were compared, some of the worst expectations of the mismatch theorists were being realized by the black workers. It was obvious that while the homes of many white blue-collar workers had followed the exodus of these jobs to the suburbs, the homes of the black blue-collar workers remained in the city. A large number of black men had to commute from central city to suburb for these jobs. The black women took more advantage of jobs in the CBD, but even among black women, there was a small net outflow of commuters from central city to suburb in all skill categories. Even though the CBD has helped the employment situation for black women and some young better-educated black men, it has not supplied the jobs necessary to meet the demand of central city blacks.

Generally, characteristics of the CBD or SMSA labor forces explain more variance in occupational standing than differences in black-white educational attainment. Education explains a relatively minor part of the variance among men, but it explains a moderate part of the variance among women. The percent using public transportation explains a relatively minor part of the variance for women.

The limitation to testing on a cross-sectional basis with CBD data put severe constraints on this study. Some of the conclusions are supported by strong and clearly interpretable evidence, as in the case of the differential impact on black men and women. Other conclusions are provisional, and await testing with longitudinal data. This study provides a benchmark which will be even more valuable when longitudinal census data become available after 1980.

Longitudinal data will allow more causal analysis in the relationship between occupational, locational, and racial variables. More sophisticated statistical models can be used with longitudinal data, and the theoretical issue of time-ordering is easier to delineate. With the data to be made available from the 1980 Census, there should be evidence to show whether the seeds of change noticed in this study have germinated. Have the black women who entered at the lower ranks of clerical workers advanced upwards? Has education paid off for young blacks in bringing greater job opportunities in the CBD? Are black clerical workers less segregated residentially than other black workers? Not only will better data be available, but the longer time-frame should show which trends have matured or dominated.

## Implications

Manpower policy makers have a twofold problem in light of this data. They must plan to make jobs available to meet the skills of the people, and they must train the people with the necessary skills to fill the available jobs. Linking supply and demand is not an easy task.

In the training of workers, there has been some talk of "overeducation." Should we have open enrollment programs or affirmative action programs if college degrees have declining usefulness and value in the job market? There are two sides to this issue. Some people with bachelor's or master's degrees are overqualified for many of the office jobs that are open. Stories of job applicants hiding these credentials verify that. But there is another kind of college student whose high school preparation is poor or average, and who gets into college through affirmative action or open enrollment programs. The high school diploma might not be enough to make persons of this sort readily employable in white-collar jobs, but two or four years of college education might upgrade their skills to the point that they would be sought after in a white-collar labor market.

Critics such as Harry Braverman see a plot on the part of businessmen to degrade the white-collar workforce by structuring the jobs in such a way that low-skilled, low-paid, relatively temporary labor can do most of the work. Other critics, recognizing a change in the number and composition of white-collar jobs, are less pessimistic in their interpretation. The results of this study suggest that the white-collar job is serving the same function for many of the recent urban migrants that the blue-collar job provided for the earlier immigrants. The trend is not without its special difficulties in its differential impact on men and women and its exclusion of poorly educated blacks, but it has its benefits in providing stepping stones into the mainstream of economic life for many blacks.

It is too simple to say that most of the job opportunities open to blacks through the expansion of offices are peripheral, low-paying, and unstable positions. Within the CBD labor force, there are various segments into which blacks are slowly filtering. The first-generation and sometimes the second-generation urban blacks can only reach the lower plateaus of this segmented labor market. The white-collar job is not the instant, stepping-stone to success, but it may lay the foundation for advancement by future generations.

Manpower training programs of agencies or companies must target on specific skills. We must not expect the impossible from these programs. In an era where there is little growth in the semi-skilled and low-skilled jobs typically held by men, and when many of these jobs are leaving the central city, it is hard to find the appropriate occupations into which these men can fit. Clerical training programs have been more successful. Without getting into the debate of why clerical jobs are filled mostly by women, there is an increasing amount of variation in clerical job types that is bringing men into such positions as data processors, computer operators, and clerks. The computer and other mechanized office functions have changed many job descriptions. The clerical workforce contains fewer of the stereotyped secretarial jobs with people sitting at a typewriter all day. Part of this stereotype is that this worker should be a woman. As changing job descriptions help to destroy the stereotype, men will probably fill many more of the clerical positions.

Economic development programs have to consider the location of jobs to satisfy the needs of industry and ensure a sufficient supply of labor. Public policy makers are less involved than formerly in massive downtown renewal efforts. Usually only a small amount of government seed money is necessary to draw a lot of private capital. But whether the decision is public or private, there ought to be a recognition that massive downtown renewal will not work in every city. Regional or national centers require a concentration of offices, hotels, etc. that other cities do not need. Even national and regional centers have overbuilt their CBDs in recent years. Many medium sized cities have arenas or convention centers, in imitation of larger cities, that are inadequately used.

Advocates of downtown development have argued that it is necessary to keep the "heart" of the city alive so that it can pump lifeblood into the city by the jobs and income it provides. Was the vast amount of public and private resources worth it, especially in terms of its impact on black employment? The "heart" analogy appears exaggerated since CBDs supply only a fraction of jobs in the metropolitan areas. But if CBD renewal had not taken place and the CBD were allowed to decay, the black employment picture might well be worse today. Assuming that blacks would have continued to concentrate residentially in inner-city areas, they would have had less access to job locations. The renewed CBD has given the black woman a foothold in the labor market of the city. The same statement cannot be repeated about the black male, except that even here there are some reasons for optimism about the future.

Economic development planners ought to give special concern to industrial pockets or parks in the central city. This would help supply jobs to those blacks who cannot fit into white-collar positions. Governments can encourage such developments by land preparation, rehabilitation subsidies, tax abatements, and investment tax credits targeted on areas of high unemployment. Generally, cities have pockets of land near rivers or railroads that is suitable for such redevelopment. Price equilibrium forces may make such space attractive, particularly to smaller manufacturing companies. Suburban land and construction costs have risen rapidly, and vacancy rates in central cities have slowed or pushed manufacturing space rentals into a decline.

While CBD and central city economic development efforts may help the blacks in the labor market, they will not become a panacea for all the problems or do away with dependency on suburban jobs. Hopefully the black population could disperse with the jobs, but that will be a slow process.

One increasing source of opposition to CBD development programs and to economic development programs in general is from neighborhood groups fighting for their share of scarce government funds. They respond to the argument that job development is necessary to keep income flowing into the city by saying that without decent neighborhoods and basic services provided to neighborhoods, no one will want to live in them anyway. These neighborhood advocates can often point to the newly built skyscrapers of the CBD from the windows of their homes, and blame the downtown interests for using up scarce resources. They have a point. But a balance must be struck whereby a sufficient flow of income must flow into the city, while neighborhoods have some resources for rehabitation.

Changes in the CBD are having an important impact on surrounding ghetto areas, or the area of transition, as Burgess called it. Many factors may contribute to a stable and renewed area of transition: a lower population density, a stable supply of jobs nearby, the removal of truck and commuter traffic to the CBD off the local streets, the vertical rather than the horizontal expansion of the CBD, the elimination of blight in the CBD, the return of some middle class workers to redeveloped pockets near the CBD, and the slowing of the migratory process to cities.

CBD renewal has replaced blight with clean and often impressive buildings and surroundings. The CBD has shed some of its manufacturing, food processing, and wholesaling functions which produced smoke, heavy truck traffic, and other unsightly or unseemly side effects. These physical improvements make the surrounding residential areas more attractive for redevelopment.

While these physical changes certainly affect the area of transition, the largest question mark regarding the future of the area of transition is whether we will have a permanent poverty class locked in inner-city residential areas. Will the area of transition house the marginal workers of whom the dual labor market theorists speak, who are trapped in low-paying, dead-end, intermittent jobs? Will the last large groups that entered the city before the migratory flows slowed down and we entered a replacement rather than a growth labor market be the ones trapped at the bottom? Will the blacks, in particular, get trapped by a chain of interaction effects between residential, employment, educational, and discriminatory factors? If we were to have this permanent poverty class, the fate of the area of transition would be sealed. It would be wrong simply to assume that the more recent migrant groups would have the same experience as the earlier migrant groups and to dismiss the possibilities raised here. This study shows some blacks moving into the middle class. But this could bring increasing class division between the blacks who have made it and the blacks who have not.

As far as the direct impact of CBD renewal on black employment, the results of this study are mixed. Outside the South it has had a beneficial impact on the employment of black women, and even in the South there are some hopeful beginnings of better employment for them. CBD renewal generally has not had a beneficial impact on black men, although here too there are some hopeful signs that better-educated young blacks are getting jobs there. As long as the male bears a stigma in our society for not being a successful provider, this differential impact on employment by sex in the CBD may contribute to stress in the black family. If the black male finds difficulty in all sectors of the metropolitan labor market, while the black woman can get a good job nearby in the CBD, it could bring frustration to the male breadwinner.

Looking at the larger context with the information used to examine the mismatch hypothesis, a dismal picture of black labor market and residential patterns emerges. While blacks have made inroads into CBD, central city, and suburban labor markets, the cumulative effect has not brought black unemployment levels down from uncomfortably high rates relative to whites. A significant black middle class is emerging, and if they choose to remain in inner-city areas, they could help to renovate and stabilize part of the area of transition. But many are still unemployed and underemployed, and the presence of large numbers of them in the area of transition would make renewal very difficult.

In addition to the problem of access to jobs, it is evident that blacks in blue-collar jobs have not dispersed residentially to suburbs with their jobs as whites have done. If they are the "outsiders" residentially, their assimilation into the labor market is bound to be slow.

While the renewed CBD has opened some opportunities for blacks and offers promise of other opportunities, it is but one piece of a large puzzle. The CBD will not be the salvation of the black community but it has had, on the whole, a moderately beneficial impact.

## Notes

1. Peter M. Blau and Otis Dudley Duncan, *The American Occupational Structure* (New York: John Wiley & Sons, 1967), p. 425.

# Appendices

# Detailed CBD Occupations by Race and Sex in 32

| | Male White | Female White | Male Black | Female Black |
|---|---|---|---|---|
| **Professional & Technical** | | | | |
| Accountants | 45100 | 9200 | 1300 | 1100 |
| Architects | 3600 | 300 | 0 | 0 |
| Computer Programmers | 5500 | 2800 | 400 | 0 |
| Computer Systems Analysts & Specialists | 4800 | 900 | 100 | 100 |
| Civil Engineers | 11900 | 200 | 200 | 0 |
| Electrical Engineers | 9100 | 700 | 200 | 0 |
| Industrial Engineers | 5600 | 200 | 0 | 0 |
| Engineers, Miscellaneous | 13500 | 200 | 0 | 0 |
| Lawyers & Judges | 39600 | 2900 | 600 | 200 |
| Librarians & Archivists | 1200 | 1700 | 0 | 100 |
| Mathematical Specialists | 1900 | 700 | 100 | 0 |
| Life & Physical Scientists | 2600 | 500 | 200 | 200 |
| Personnel & Labor Relations | 12400 | 7200 | 800 | 600 |
| Physicians & Dentists | 8700 | 900 | 200 | 100 |
| Nurses, Dieticians & Therapists | 800 | 6700 | 0 | 1000 |
| Health Technicians | 600 | 1200 | 100 | 600 |
| Social Scientists | 6100 | 1400 | 200 | 100 |
| Social & Recreation Workers | 4400 | 6200 | 700 | 1300 |
| Teachers | 5300 | 6900 | 500 | 1000 |
| Technicians & Draftsmen | 17900 | 1600 | 700 | 300 |
| Editors & Reporters | 6600 | 3700 | 100 | 100 |
| Professional & Technical, Miscellaneous | 26900 | 9400 | 900 | 900 |
| Total | 234100 | 65500 | 7300 | 7700 |
| | | | | |
| **Managers & Administrators** | | | | |
| Bank Officers & Financial Managers | 24300 | 3500 | 400 | 0 |
| Buyers | 6400 | 4700 | 100 | 0 |
| Officials & Administrators; Public Administration | 13600 | 2400 | 800 | 200 |
| Office Managers | 5800 | 3900 | 100 | 0 |
| Sales Managers, Except Retail | 9000 | 300 | 200 | 0 |
| Managers & Administrators | 73800 | 12100 | 1200 | 500 |
| Miscellaneous, Managers & Administrators | 26400 | 6100 | 1800 | 1000 |
| Total | 159300 | 33000 | 4600 | 1700 |
| | | | | |
| **Sales Workers** | | | | |
| Insurance Agents, Brokers & Underwriters | 22600 | 4300 | 900 | 100 |
| Stock & Bond Salesmen | 13800 | 1300 | 100 | 0 |
| Sales Representatives, Wholesale Trade | 11900 | 1000 | 100 | 0 |
| Sales Clerks, Retail Trade | 16900 | 36900 | 1700 | 5000 |
| Miscellaneous, Sales Workers | 29700 | 11600 | 700 | 700 |
| Total | 94900 | 55100 | 3500 | 5800 |
| | | | | |
| **High-level Clerical Workers** | | | | |
| Computer & Peripheral Equipment Operators | 4700 | 1500 | 300 | 200 |
| Key Punch Operators | 1700 | 12800 | 100 | 3700 |
| Secretaries | 5000 | 128000 | 0 | 8600 |
| Stenographers | 800 | 7700 | 0 | 1000 |
| Miscellaneous, High Level Clerical | 900 | 2300 | 500 | 600 |
| Total | 13100 | 152300 | 900 | 14100 |

# Non-Southern Cities, 1970

|  | Male White | Female White | Male Black | Female Black |
|---|---|---|---|---|
| **Low-level Clerical Workers** | | | | |
| Bank Tellers | 2300 | 7500 | 100 | 200 |
| Bookkeepers | 11100 | 39700 | 900 | 4300 |
| Telegraph, Telephone Operators | 1200 | 24000 | 0 | 6300 |
| Estimators & Investigators | 9100 | 7600 | 500 | 1400 |
| File Clerks | 4200 | 18100 | 1000 | 3600 |
| Receptionists | 300 | 10400 | 100 | 1700 |
| Statistical Clerks | 3600 | 10700 | 500 | 2000 |
| Typists | 3300 | 53100 | 900 | 11400 |
| Miscellaneous, Low-level Clerical | 29900 | 55100 | 2700 | 10400 |
| Total | 65000 | 226200 | 6700 | 41300 |
| | | | | |
| **Office-associated, Clerical Jobs** | | | | |
| Mail, Messengers, Office Boys | 8100 | 4800 | 4100 | 1000 |
| Postal Clerks | 6900 | 1800 | 3900 | 2800 |
| Miscellaneous, Office Associated | 5900 | 100 | 1200 | 0 |
| Total | 20900 | 6700 | 9200 | 3800 |
| | | | | |
| **Clerical, Non-office** | | | | |
| Cashiers | 2400 | 10700 | 100 | 1600 |
| Stock Clerks | 4500 | 2700 | 1400 | 700 |
| Miscellaneous, Clerical, Non-office | 20500 | 29400 | 1400 | 5400 |
| Total | 27400 | 42800 | 2900 | 7700 |
| | | | | |
| **Craftsmen** | | | | |
| Construction | 17300 | 200 | 2900 | 0 |
| Other Craftsmen | 87700 | 9500 | 6200 | 1100 |
| Total | 105000 | 9700 | 9100 | 1100 |
| | | | | |
| **Operatives** | | | | |
| Transport Operatives | 21300 | 600 | 6100 | 100 |
| Miscellaneous | 23600 | 30300 | 5300 | 7700 |
| Total | 44900 | 30900 | 11400 | 7800 |
| | | | | |
| **Laborers** | | | | |
| Miscellaneous | 16600 | 2700 | 7300 | 800 |
| | | | | |
| **Service Workers** | | | | |
| Cleaning Service | 14100 | 12100 | 8100 | 6000 |
| Food Service | 14400 | 20400 | 3100 | 5600 |
| Health Service | 300 | 4300 | 200 | 1900 |
| Personal Service | 8100 | 8900 | 1800 | 1700 |
| Police | 20200 | 1600 | 1700 | 200 |
| Other Protective Service | 10700 | 800 | 1900 | 100 |
| Private Household | 0 | 800 | 0 | 1500 |
| Miscellaneous Service | 900 | 700 | 500 | 400 |
| Total | 68700 | 49600 | 17300 | 17400 |

The estimated standard errors of these statistics, taken from the 1 in 100 sample of the Public Use Sample, are presented in Chapter 5, footnote 2.

# Detailed CBD Occupations by Race and Sex in 22

| | Male White | Female White | Male Black | Female Black |
|---|---|---|---|---|
| **Professional & Technical** | | | | |
| Accountants | 17100 | 4000 | 200 | 100 |
| Architects | 1200 | 0 | 0 | 0 |
| Computer Programmers | 2100 | 1300 | 0 | 300 |
| Computer Systems Analysts & Specialists | 1200 | 200 | 100 | 0 |
| Civil Engineers | 3100 | 0 | 0 | 0 |
| Electrical Engineers | 3400 | 0 | 0 | 0 |
| Industrial Engineers | 1600 | 100 | 0 | 0 |
| Engineers, Miscellaneous | 4100 | 100 | 0 | 0 |
| Lawyers & Judges | 13500 | 600 | 0 | 0 |
| Librarians & Archivists | 100 | 500 | 0 | 0 |
| Mathematical Specialists | 200 | 200 | 0 | 0 |
| Life & Physical Scientists | 2600 | 0 | 100 | 0 |
| Personnel & Labor Relations | 4200 | 3100 | 100 | 200 |
| Physicians & Dentists | 4400 | 200 | 0 | 0 |
| Nurses, Dieticians & Therapists | 200 | 4600 | 0 | 500 |
| Health Technicians | 300 | 1700 | 100 | 500 |
| Social Scientists | 2100 | 0 | 100 | 0 |
| Social & Recreation Workers | 600 | 1800 | 400 | 200 |
| Teachers | 1500 | 2800 | 300 | 400 |
| Technicians & Draftsmen | 6300 | 1100 | 200 | 100 |
| Editors | 1900 | 1000 | 200 | 100 |
| Professional & Technical, Miscellaneous | 8900 | 4000 | 500 | 400 |
| Total | 80600 | 27300 | 2300 | 2800 |
| | | | | |
| **Managers & Administrators** | | | | |
| Bank Officers & Financial Managers | 6700 | 1800 | 200 | 200 |
| Buyers | 2300 | 1500 | 100 | 0 |
| Officials & Administrators; Public Administration | 3600 | 1000 | 100 | 0 |
| Office Managers | 2100 | 1500 | 0 | 0 |
| Sales Managers, Except Retail | 2800 | 500 | 0 | 0 |
| Managers & Administrators | 30000 | 4300 | 800 | 300 |
| Managers & Administrators, Miscellaneous | 10300 | 2500 | 300 | 0 |
| Total | 57800 | 13100 | 1500 | 500 |
| | | | | |
| **Sales Workers** | | | | |
| Insurance Agents, Brokers & Underwriters | 6000 | 1700 | 100 | 0 |
| Stock & Bond Salesmen | 4300 | 200 | 0 | 100 |
| Sales Representatives, Wholesale Trade | 6300 | 800 | 0 | 100 |
| Sales Clerks, Retail Trade | 7100 | 18700 | 600 | 2300 |
| Sales Workers, Miscellaneous | 13100 | 3900 | 300 | 200 |
| Total | 36800 | 25300 | 1000 | 2700 |
| | | | | |
| **High-level Clerical Workers** | | | | |
| Computer & Peripheral Equipment Operators | 2000 | 900 | 200 | 100 |
| Key Punch Operators | 300 | 4100 | 0 | 500 |
| Secretaries | 1400 | 47100 | 0 | 1400 |
| Stenographers | 200 | 3500 | 0 | 400 |
| High-level Clerical, Miscellaneous | 900 | 3800 | 0 | 100 |
| Total | 4800 | 59400 | 200 | 2500 |

# Southern Cities, 1970

| | Male White | Female White | Male Black | Female Black |
|---|---|---|---|---|
| **Low-level Clerical Workers** | | | | |
| Bank Tellers | 600 | 2900 | 300 | 100 |
| Bookkeepers | 3500 | 16200 | 200 | 700 |
| Telegraph, Telephone Operators | 400 | 10000 | 100 | 4000 |
| Estimators & Investigators | 3000 | 2400 | 0 | 100 |
| File Clerks | 1400 | 5700 | 400 | 800 |
| Receptionists | 0 | 3400 | 0 | 100 |
| Statistical Clerks | 1500 | 4200 | 0 | 200 |
| Typists | 1000 | 15400 | 200 | 1400 |
| Low-level Clerical, Miscellaneous | 11800 | 24300 | 1100 | 3700 |
| Total | 23200 | 81100 | 2300 | 11100 |
| **Office-associated, Clerical Jobs** | | | | |
| Mail, Messengers, Office Boys | 2500 | 1500 | 900 | 300 |
| Postal Clerks | 3700 | 1100 | 2900 | 1600 |
| Office-associated, Miscellaneous | 2600 | 100 | 1200 | 0 |
| Total | 8800 | 2700 | 5000 | 1900 |
| **Clerical, Non-office** | | | | |
| Cashiers | 600 | 5200 | 0 | 1700 |
| Stock Clerks | 2100 | 900 | 700 | 500 |
| Miscellaneous, Clerical, Non-office | 6500 | 12500 | 1000 | 700 |
| Total | 9200 | 18600 | 1700 | 2900 |
| **Craftsmen** | | | | |
| Construction | 8500 | 200 | 1200 | 0 |
| Other Craftsmen | 35200 | 2300 | 2300 | 500 |
| Total | 43700 | 2500 | 3500 | 500 |
| **Operatives** | | | | |
| Transport Operatives | 8700 | 300 | 6000 | 300 |
| Miscellaneous | 9900 | 8800 | 4300 | 3500 |
| Total | 18600 | 9100 | 10300 | 3800 |
| **Laborers** | | | | |
| Miscellaneous | 6500 | 800 | 6400 | 200 |
| **Service Workers** | | | | |
| Cleaning Service | 3300 | 2300 | 6500 | 4800 |
| Food Service | 3000 | 5900 | 4100 | 5500 |
| Health Service | 200 | 2900 | 300 | 2500 |
| Personal Service | 2500 | 3300 | 1500 | 1400 |
| Police | 6600 | 200 | 400 | 0 |
| Other Protective Service | 7400 | 600 | 500 | 100 |
| Private Household | 0 | 100 | 100 | 800 |
| Miscellaneous Service | 200 | 600 | 100 | 200 |
| Total | 23200 | 15900 | 13500 | 15300 |

The estimated standard errors of these statistics, taken from the 1 in 100 sample of the Public Use Sample, are presented in Chapter 5, footnote 2.

## APPENDIX C
# The Multivariate Analysis

### Choice of the Independent Variables

The Varimax orthogonal rotations in the SPSS program package were used to factor analyze the key indicators of the occupational structure of the SMSA and CBD.[1] Three independent and clearly interpretable factors emerged: manufacturing, office work, and government employment.

Factor analysis was used in choosing the key indicators of the occupational structure of the SMSA and the CBD. In the zero order correlations, the percent of workers in construction has the largest correlations with black occupational standing. The sign of the correlations indicates an inverse relation between percent construction and black standing. These correlations are in the range of .50 to .60. But in the factoring, percent construction loaded on many factors, indicating that it is not simply measuring the impact of opportunity in the construction industry for blacks. It apparently also indicates something about the occupational stability of the city. For instance, it could indicate a city which is in the process of shifting to more and more white-collar jobs, if the construction is for office or commercial purposes. Construction could also be an indicator of the economic health of the city. Percent construction correlates at -.70 with percent manufacturing and +.52 with percent retailing in the city. Because it is an indicator of more than just the impact of opportunity in one industry, it was not included in the regression.

Another strong indicator of black occupational standing which loads on various factors is retailing. Its highest loading is on the same factor with office work, but with opposite signs. (The zero order correlation between office concentration in the CBD and percent retailing in the CBD is -.61). There is a strong inverse relation between the two. Perhaps the demand for office space has simply pushed out retailing from the center of the city. Offices derive a greater advantage from centrality, and by building up land prices, they squeeze out the retail stores which no longer depend so much on a public transportation mode.

Factor analysis aided in the choice of indicators of the ecological and demographic characteristics of cities. Table 7.2 showed the zero order correlations of many of these characteistics. In factor analysis, factors emerged centered around the percentage of public transportation users and percent black in the SMSA. As would be expected from the correlation matrix, the variables which loaded on these factors differed in the southern and non-southern states. Table C.1 shows these factors. In trial regression runs, factor scores were used, and they did explain a little more variance than the simple indicators of public transportation users and percent black. But since different variables loaded on the factors in the South and non-South, theoretical problems arose in comparing them. So the simple indicators, which always emerged with the highest loadings on the factors anyway, were used instead of the factor scores in the final regression run.

## The Linearity Assumption

To check that there were linear relationships between the variables, scattergrams were run to show the zero-order relationships between key independent and dependent variables. Similar studies had found it necessary to use the logs of certain variables such as population size. But the scattergrams in this study did not reveal any curvilinear relationships.

## The Interpretation of Beta Coefficients

With the CBD and SMSA data in this study, it would not be legitimate to compare the standardized "betas" directly. Such

Appendix Table C.1  Factor Analysis of SMSA Ecological and Demographic Characteristics, 1970

|  | Factor I<br>City Ecological Structure | Factor II<br>City Racial Characteristics |
|---|---|---|
| Non-Southern Cities |  |  |
| City Size | .894 | −.041 |
| Percent Black | .506 | .551 |
| Percent Public Transportation | .681 | .232 |
| Black Centrality | .031 | .469 |
| Black Segregation | .110 | .042 |
| Southern Cities |  |  |
| City Size | .182 | .053 |
| Percent Black | .371 | .722 |
| Percent Public Transportation | .957 | .272 |
| Black Centrality | .052 | .644 |
| Black Segregation | −.530 | .062 |

direct comparison depends on a constant ratio of the standard deviation of the independent variable to the standard deviation of the dependent variable in the regression equations.

It is legitimate, according to Ronald Schoenberg, to compare the results of a crude comparison within each model or equation with the use of betas.[2] This means that a rough ordering of the effects contributed by the independent variables may be compared. We might say that percent manufacturing, for example, always explains more variance than any of the other variables in the equations for different regions or sexes. Such comparisons can be done only with standardized coefficients. The regressions in this study have three characteristics, which, according to Schoenberg, lend confidence in making such comparisons. First, and most importantly, the standard deviations of the dependent variables are very similar between regions. The standard deviations of all variables in the regression analysis appear in Table C.2. The only significant variations among these appears in the measures of female relative minority income, and these are not important variables in this study. Secondly, the standard deviations of the independent variables do not differ greatly across regions. The very significant exceptions here are the measures of public transportation use. Finally, the same measure and units of measure were used on all variables.

## The Unsuitability of Other Multivariate Statistical Models

Consideration was given to the use of path models, especially the standardized path model and the Blalock model. Examples were tried with the data in the study. They were not employed in the final analysis for several reasons. First, the nature of relationships in southern and non-southern cities was so different, that separate models would have to be used for each region. But the number of cases (22 southern cities and 32 non-southern cities) was not enough to get many significant coefficients in the models. Secondly, it was impossible to get a hard and fast recursive time-ordering of variables. An example of this is the relation of the availability of public transportation to occupational standing. Does public transportation lead to better occupational standing, or is it merely a reflection of occupational standing in that the lowest income users are

**Appendix Table C.2  Standard Deviations and Means of Variables Used in the Regression Analysis**

| | All Cities | Non-South | South |
|---|---|---|---|
| **Relative Minority Income** | | | |
| Male CBD Workers | 6.86 (49.57) | 5.37 (53.07) | 5.51 (44.48) |
| Female CBD Workers | 9.65 (76.14) | 7.28 (82.07) | 5.11 (67.50) |
| Male SMSA Workers | 7.09 (60.15) | 4.52 (64.80) | 5.28 (54.27) |
| Female SMSA Workers | 10.42 (79.62) | 6.11 (86.84) | 4.90 (69.12) |
| **Index of Occupational Dissimilarity** | | | |
| Male CBD Workers | 6.98 (44.42) | 4.95 (40.22) | 4.58 (50.53) |
| Female CBD Workers | 12.01 (28.56) | 8.13 (21.23) | 8.12 (39.22) |
| **Public Transportation Users** | | | |
| All SMSA Workers | 5.59 (7.54) | 6.01 (8.74) | 4.50 (5.79) |
| Male CBD Workers | 13.97 (14.33) | 16.28 (18.62) | 5.71 (8.08) |
| Female CBD Workers | 20.22 (32.01) | 21.18 (40.38) | 11.97 (21.32) |
| **Relative Black Education** | | | |
| Male | 9.57 (63.06) | 8.34 (65.67) | 10.16 (59.26) |
| Female | 8.39 (68.18) | 6.59 (70.57) | 9.61 (64.70) |
| Percent Black in SMSA | 7.86 (13.62) | 5.89 (10.59) | 8.37 (18.03) |
| SMSA Percent Manufacturing | 9.29 (25.00) | 9.30 (28.07) | 7.40 (20.95) |
| SMSA Percent Government Jobs | 4.22 (6.17) | 4.58 (6.09) | 3.73 (6.29) |
| SMSA Percent Female Clerical | 3.56 (37.87) | 3.39 (38.59) | 3.63 (36.83) |
| CBD Office Concentration Index | 4.01 (28.58) | 4.27 (29.34) | 3.41 (27.48) |
| CBD Percent Government Jobs | 6.39 (11.62) | 7.26 (11.96) | 4.97 (11.13) |

Means appear in parentheses.

forced to use it? Apparent mutual causation or feedback occurs with many of the variables in the study.

The final reason is that some of the data is not refined enough for use in elaborate mathematical models. The present mathematical models are extremely sensitive to error in measurement. Given the usual problem of error in census data, there is the added problem in this study of a loose definition of geographical areas, especially the CBD.

## Notes

1. Norman H. Nie, Dale H. Bent and C. Hadlai Hull, *Statistical Package for the Social Sciences* (New York: McGraw-Hill, 1970).

2. Ronald Schoenberg, "Strategies for Meaningful Comparison," in *Sociological Methodology*, ed. Herbert Costner (San Francisco: Jossey-Bass, 1972), p. 21.

# Index

# ABOUT THE AUTHOR

Brian J. O'Connell is Assistant Professor of Sociology, St. John's University. He has contributed articles to the *Journal of the American Institute of Planners*, *Review of Religious Research*, *Sociological Analysis*, and *America*. He lectures frequently on urban labor issues and neighborhood development.